A Cop for Christ

A Cop for Christ

The Dramatic True Story of Mike DiSanza of the NYPD

Written with Liz Hinds

Hodder & Stoughton

LONDON SYDNEY AUCKLAND

British Library Cataloguing in Publication Data
A record for this book is available from the British Library

ISBN 0 340 78519 5

Typeset by Avon Dataset Ltd, Bidford-on-Avon, Warks

Printed and bound in Great Britain by
Clays Ltd, St Ives plc

Hodder & Stoughton
A Division of Hodder Headline Ltd
338 Euston Road
London NW1 3BH

Foreword

In the Godhead we have the Father, the Son and the Holy Ghost, three persons in one God. Each one as much God as the other. In New York City, we had three police departments: Street, Transit and Housing. All three had the same police power. I was a member of the Transit Police. Ten years back all three merged and became one. They are now one police. NYPD.

This book is dedicated to: Jesus; my angels; my wife Ann, who is my forever police partner and who as a cop's wife lives every second of this most dangerous job; and last but not least, every police officer in New York City – who are some of the greatest men and women I have known – cops in America, and cops all around the world.

I wrote this book to show you God's sustaining power in any situation in your life, even when bullets are flying around you. Hang in there! God's gonna take us all the way through with Jesus.

Introduction

Tension had been mounting all evening. The sticky heat of a long summer's night in New York City meant trouble on the streets, you could bet your last dollar on it. On many blocks, on many street corners, groups of restless New Yorkers gathered. The air was full of suppressed anger. Years of poverty, fear and frustration had created generations of downtrodden people, and polluted, airless conditions have a habit of bringing things to a head.

The police were out in force. Something sinister and dangerous was imminent.

Not long after midnight it began. A man was arrested. His crime was unimportant; he was simply the trigger. He became the cause – he gave people a reason to react.

This wasn't gang warfare, one group of people with a particular allegiance or ethnic background against another. This was the hippie generation, led on by a handful of subversives, rising up against authority, represented by the police.

The crowds who had been scattered throughout 42nd Street and Times Square gathered together, their fury building with each moment that passed. They turned on the police, swearing and screaming abuse. The first bottle to be thrown was quickly followed by others, and then bricks and any other missiles to hand.

The police responded in the only way possible, meeting violence with strong resistance, using nightsticks to protect themselves and to hold back the rioters. They were still unable to prevent a number of patrolmen being injured in the scuffles.

Back-up units were summoned, but by then it was too late. Nothing could now stop the crowds, who numbered near a thousand, from storming the streets.

It was several hours before order was restored, before a peace of some sort was established. Maybe fatigue had something to do with it, or maybe the crowds just ran out of steam. They'd been able to give voice to their frustrations for a while, but in the end both the rioters and the authorities were left as bitter as the acrid smoke from the burning cars.

I was a young cop in those days, experiencing my first riot in my first summer on the streets. I'd read about riots in the papers, seen them on television, but nothing had prepared me for this.

This wasn't like TV. This was real. I could see the anger in people; I could feel the hatred coming out of them; I could understand their fears, their desperation.

Amid the noise and violence, the arrests and injuries, my overriding emotion was one of terrible fear. I remember thinking, 'Is this what I'm gonna be facing all my working life?'

Over the next twenty-two years, I saw more riots and all sorts of unspeakable crimes. I also saw how many policemen responded to the suffering they saw in the only way they knew, by burying their emotions and becoming hard. But God had other plans for me. Thank God, I found Jesus.

Chapter 1

I was ready for him. I stood with my knees slightly bent, my body angled towards my opponent and a piece of wood gripped firmly in my hands.

'You're going to have to do better than that, Charlie, if you wanna get me outta here,' I yelled.

'Just you wait, Mikey, see what you can do with this.'

'Oh yeah? Come on, then.'

I grinned. Let him try, I thought. I was ten years old. I had all the confidence in the world.

At the other end of the concrete school-yard, Charlie began his pitch, his face distorted with determination. His last ball had hit the wall behind my knees, well outside the large chalk square that represented home plate, but this time he was sure he was going to get a strike, I knew it. And I was just as determined to stop him.

Charlie completed his pitch. His timing was perfect. The small rubber Spading ball shot through the air straight towards the large chalk square ... and straight towards the old broom-handle I was using as a bat. I drew it back and swung it forward to hit the Spading, which soared high into the sky. I put up my hand to shield my eyes from the sun as I watched the ball's progress. Charlie turned and was watching it too, as he started to run, following the line through the air, hoping to make a catch. Our eyes continued to follow the ball as it started its descent. Charlie speeded up and then came to a sudden halt. His way was blocked by the solid brick wall of the old catholic church which bordered one side of the school-yard. The ball landed on the roof and bounced into the guttering.

I walked over to join Charlie, and we stood together and looked up at the roof. We'd pooled our money to buy the ball the day before. It was the only ball we had, and we had no more money.

'We gotta get it back.'

'Yeah,' Charlie agreed.

'Look, if you give me a shimmy, I should be able to get up there. It's not too high.'

We walked along beside the wall, studying it until we found the most likely-looking section with the most footholds, and then Charlie bent over and formed his hands into a cradle. I put my left foot in, then felt around the rough brickwork of the wall until I found an edge I could grip. With Charlie pushing and me pulling myself up, I could just reach the edge of the flat rooftop. I gave it a tug to test its safety.

'It's okay, it'll hold me. Just give me another bunk up.'

Down below, Charlie grunted. It was a hot day. I could hear him take a deep breath and then he straightened up as far as he could, supporting my weight. It was enough. With a final heave I pulled myself up on to the roof, and what I saw there, I tell you, I would have given a plate of my mother's meatballs for.

'Charlie, gold!' I yelled.

'What? What you talking about, Mikey?'

'Here, catch, Charlie.'

One by one, and then two by two, I showered Charlie with balls, the legacy of generations of kids who'd played softball in the school-yard. We'd stumbled across treasure.

'Wow!'

I sent Charlie scuttling all over the place collecting up the balls that I bounced down from above, until at last the roof was clear. We must have had at least a hundred balls. I scrambled down and we hunted around until we found a box to store them in. When we'd done, we stood back and looked at our plunder. There were enough balls there to last all summer at least. We grinned at each other and then, suddenly, Charlie remembered something.

'Hey, the ball went out of play so that means you're out.'

I was about to argue with him when we heard the squeal of the school-yard gate opening. We looked around. There were two gangs, one black, one white, of youths coming into the yard. We didn't know what was going on but it didn't look good. We hurriedly pushed our box into a corner behind a shed and crouched down beside it.

When the yard was full – there must have been two hundred there altogether – one of the youths took a heavy metal chain and padlocked the gate. We knew then that whatever was happening, no one was going to leave until it was over.

The rival gangs lined up on opposite sides of the yard, and there was a nervous silence. The air smelled of sweat and fear. Then two of the older youths strode into the centre of the yard. They each raised an arm and held it in the air for a moment before dropping it. This must have been the signal the rest were waiting for. The two gangs charged. They laid into each other using knives, chains, baseball bats, the sharp pointed metal of car aerials, or anything they had been able to lay their hands on that would cause damage to their enemy.

Charlie and I cowered in the corner, huddled together, watching all this, not daring to move or say a word, thankful that no one had spotted us.

After what seemed like hours but was probably only ten minutes, we heard the sound of sirens wailing as police cars approached the yard. We figured some passers-by must have seen the fight and called the police. The gang members heard the sirens too, over the screaming and yelling, and those that could still walk struggled to climb over the chain-link fence to escape. Others were too badly injured to get up off the ground, where they lay bleeding or semi-conscious.

When it was all over and the last body had been taken away in an ambulance or a squad car, Charlie and I stood up. We didn't say anything, just picked up the box of balls between us and made our way slowly back home.

That incident, my first real encounter with violence, had a profoundly shocking effect on me. For three months afterwards I shut myself away, refusing to leave the apartment. I went straight to school in the morning and came straight home again at night. My mom and dad couldn't understand it.

They asked me, 'What's the matter with you, Mike?'

But I didn't want to talk about it, I couldn't talk about it. Charlie and I had seen the kind of things no one should see when they're only ten years old.

The balls, the treasure we had found, stayed unused in their box that summer.

Perhaps Charlie and I were lucky to have reached ten years old without witnessing violence, living as we did in New York's notorious South Bronx. While the majority of people who lived there were families like mine and Charlie's, decent hard-working men and women who struggled to give their children a good upbringing in spite of poverty and bad conditions, there were others who chose a different life, and what Charlie and I had seen that day was an everyday part of life for many.

But not for us.

I was born in the South Bronx in 1946 to Albert and Bernadette DiSanza. They'd both been born in New York City of immigrant parents. My mom was Italian and my dad was Spanish–Italian. Economically we were at the bottom of the scale. My dad had had to leave school during the Depression, and both my parents worked in factories for very little pay. My mom was a seamstress in a sweatshop. They were hard workers but they only earned enough money to keep us fed and for the bare essentials. We were a typical Italian–Spanish family: we ate lots of spaghetti, which was cheap, and my mom's meatballs, which were the best. We didn't have a car or a television, but we had a good loving home.

The six of us – my parents, me, my twin brother Tommy, my older brother John and my little sister Laura – lived on the fifth, the top floor of an apartment building on 148th Street. In any street on the Bronx, there are maybe ten buildings on each side, each building housing thirty families. My grandparents had ten children and they all lived on the same street, so I was never short of cousins to play with.

The neighbourhood we lived in was predominantly Italian. If a family moved out, it was usually another Italian family that would move in. The Bronx was like that, split into ethnic areas. As well as the Italian quarter, there were black, Irish and Puerto Rican neighbourhoods.

Coming from a Roman Catholic family, I grew up attending St Peter's, the local Catholic church. Roman Catholicism and all its rituals played a large part in my early life. We went to confession on Saturdays and Mass on Sundays. There seemed to be rules and regulations governing everything I did. I soon learned that if I did wrong and died without making confession, I would go to hell, and that it was a terrible, terrible place. This was drummed into me and the fear of it overwhelmed me; it was always there in the back of my mind. The only way to avoid going to hell was to go to confession, and that became part of my Saturday ritual.

Like any normal kid I was constantly doing wrong during the week, and it was a real worry for me that I would have an accident and die before I had a chance to confess my sins the next Saturday.

One of the many rules I learned by heart was that it was a sin to eat meat on Fridays.

Every Sunday we'd have meatballs for dinner. My mom worked of a Saturday so she'd prepare the meatballs on Friday and freeze them – that way they'd be ready and she wouldn't have to spend a long time making them on Sunday. One day I got home from school and found that she had forgotten to put the meatballs in the freezer. Instead, she'd left them out on the kitchen table. I looked at the tray of meatballs and my mouth watered. My mom's meatballs were so good.

'She won't miss it,' I told myself, 'if I just take one.'

I put out my hand towards the tray, then I stopped.

'Nah, I shouldn't.'

I turned away, but the delicious smell filling the kitchen stopped me. I looked over my shoulder at the meatballs. I'm sure I heard them call out to me – surely it wouldn't hurt if I just took one?

I grabbed the juiciest-looking and stuffed it in my mouth. Mmm, it tasted good. But now there was a gap on the tray where my meatball had been. I figured if I moved the others around a bit no one would notice there was one missing, and I was just wiping my hands when I remembered something.

It was Friday.

A sudden cold fear gripped my stomach.

I wasn't supposed to eat meat on Fridays.

I knew if my mom found out that I'd taken a meatball she would shout at me, but she'd soon forgive me. I wasn't scared about that. No, I was scared because I'd committed a far more serious sin – the sin of eating meat on a Friday. I knew that if I died that night I'd go to hell, and just because of that one meatball. I didn't sleep that night and I was first in line for confession the next day.

When I got older, I liked to go out on the town on Saturday nights with the boys. After one Saturday night when we'd been drinking and partying, I overslept. When I woke up, I rolled over in my bed and looked at the clock. I saw it was early afternoon. I closed my eyes again and then suddenly I sat bolt upright, wide awake.

'I've missed Mass!'

The thought struck me like a thunderbolt from heaven. I'd missed Mass and that was a mortal sin. If I died before going to confession next Saturday, I would go to hell.

I couldn't go back to sleep now. I sat on the edge of the bed, trying to calm the anxious thoughts going round my head. I wondered if a hot bath would make me feel better. I got up, went to the bathroom and turned on the faucet (water tap). When the bath was full enough, I dipped my hand in to test the temperature.

'Ow!' I pulled my hand out quickly. I hadn't turned on the cold water and the bath was scalding hot. That was when it hit me. If I can't take this hot water for one second, how am I going to cope with burning for ever in hell?

I changed my mind about the bath. Instead, I pulled on some clothes and ran down the road to the rectory. I knocked impatiently on the door. When the priest opened it, he was rubbing his eyes, looking like he'd just been woken up from his Sunday afternoon nap. I blurted out, 'You gotta hear my confession, Father.'

'Why, what's the problem, Mikey? Have you killed someone?'

'No, Father, but I missed Mass this morning.'

'Is that all? Can't you wait until next Saturday to have your confession?'

'It's all right for you. If you die today, you're going to heaven. If I die today, I'm going to hell.'

This was a real concern for me. I was coming to think of God, if he existed at all, as someone who was out to get me. I had no security, no peace, no certainty of my salvation. As far as I was concerned, I was destined for hell, and there was nothing I could do about it. I was a yo-yo Christian, headed for heaven one day and hell the next. The Church told me what to do and what not to do. I knew I could never hit the mark. I was fed up with struggling and always failing, so I stopped going to confession as often.

The next time I went I began, 'Father, forgive me for I have sinned. It has been six months since my last conf–'

The words weren't out of my mouth before the good father was at my side in the confessional. He grabbed me by the shoulders and shook me.

'You didn't come here for six months?!'

I was taken by surprise by his response, but by then I had lost most of my respect for the Church so I stood up to him.

'No, I haven't been here for six months, and let me tell you why. I'm tired of coming here every week saying the same things and nothing ever changing, so I figured I'd just save it all up for six months, do it all in one go.'

The priest looked at me and his face changed. He smiled, 'Well, at least someone round here is honest!'

I often wondered what the priest thought when he listened to confessions on a Saturday. Did the idea of a young boy's stolen meatball make him chuckle? Did he ever question the rules that brought such fear into lives? Did he have any idea what guilt and anxiety were being instilled by the regulations, or what condemnation people were living under?

Eventually I gave up even on the six-monthly confessions. I stopped going to church altogether.

Chapter 2

Looking back now I can see how, even though at that time I was walking away from God, he had plans for my life right from the beginning. Over the course of about ten years, three things happened to me that I call my three miracles, three meetings that changed the course of my life. The third one was meeting Jesus; the first one happened when I was a young teenager.

Life wasn't easy for my parents, trying to raise four children. They worked long hours in tough conditions just to earn enough to keep us fed and clothed. They couldn't afford to give us pocket money. If we kids wanted a new baseball bat or a football, we knew it was no use asking Dad. He would have loved to have gone out and bought us new things, but he didn't have the money. If we wanted anything, we had to work for it.

Saturday mornings I'd shine shoes on the street corner, and every weekday, mornings and evenings, I'd deliver newspapers. On Saturdays, I also had to collect the money people owed for their papers. I earned $11 a week, and out of that I gave my dad $8. With the $3 I had left, I'd spend some and I'd save some.

One time I was saving for a baseball glove. I'd seen the one I wanted and I only needed one more dollar. I figured I'd collect the paper money, take it to the newsagent, he'd pay me and I could go right to the store and buy my glove. It was a sunny day and I was hurrying around to collect from all my customers. I'd just come out of one apartment block, and I had my head bent over checking the money and putting it in my pocket when three guys came out of the shadows. They were wearing nylon stockings over their heads. They surrounded me and pushed me into an alley and up against the wall. One of them grabbed my shirt at my neck and pressed his face into mine.

'Hand over the money, man.'

I could hear the snarl in his voice and feel his hot breath on my cheek. The smart thing would have been to do as he said and give them the money, but I wasn't feeling smart. I was angry.

'No way! I've worked all week for this,' I said, gripping my pocket tightly.

I figured the newspaper distributor wouldn't pay me if I lost his money and I really wanted that glove.

I hadn't even finished speaking before they laid into me. One by one, they landed punches on me, knocking my head from side to side. One of them had brass knuckles or something, which he smashed into my jaw breaking my teeth; another broke off a radio antenna from a nearby parked car and dug it into my ribs. They had me pinned up against the wall; I was helpless. Then one of them, the leader of the gang, I guess, pulled out a knife and moved it slowly around in front of my face before dragging it across my cheek.

Now I was really scared and bleeding badly. I knew I had to get away. I knew, if I could just get loose, that I could outrun them – I was one of the fastest runners in school – and somehow I managed to struggle free. I don't know how I did it, but I started to run and I didn't stop until I was sure I had left them well behind.

I had escaped and I still had my money, but I wasn't completely victorious. I went home, bleeding and bruised.

'Mikey, what happened to you?' my mom cried when she saw me.

'It's okay, Mom,' I said, 'I'm all right.'

I told her what had happened and she took me to the hospital, where I needed about seven stitches. But neither the doctors, with all their expertise, nor my mom, with all her love and care, could fix the real damage I suffered that day. There was one wound that no one could mend, that wasn't visible on the surface. It was far deeper than skin or even flesh; it was deep in my heart. I was filled with hatred – a great overwhelming sense of hatred. I decided there and then that I would never let anything like this happen to me ever again. I would never again be beaten up or be so frightened, and I knew what I had to do.

On a corner of our street there was a clubhouse where a lot of Italian guys hung out. They weren't yet proper Mafia but they were small-time, dabbling on the edge. It wasn't a good place to be. My mom and dad had warned me not to go near it, but I was desperate, I didn't care any more. I went down to the clubhouse. I pushed open the door and walked in. It was dark inside and it took my eyes a couple of minutes to get used to the gloom. Then I heard a voice.

'Whad'ya want, kid?'

I looked in the direction the voice came from. A big crease-faced guy was leaning against the wall. He didn't look or sound welcoming. I nearly turned and went back out, but then I remembered the beating I'd had and why I was there. I took a deep breath and said, 'I want to join your gang.'

He didn't say anything but slowly looked me up and down. Then he walked over to me. I drew myself up as far as I could and tried not to let him see my fear. He walked around me and then when he was in front of me again, he punched me in the face. The force of the unexpected blow knocked me against the wall. He shouted something into a back room and two others guys came out, and the three of them set into me. I tried fighting back, swinging punches at them; I even managed to land a few blows here and there, but it was an unequal fight. Just when I thought I was done for and I'd have to give up, I heard someone say, 'Okay, enough, leave the kid alone.'

The three guys stopped hitting me right away and stepped back. I slumped on the floor.

'Get the kid a drink and help him on to a chair,' the same voice said. I was half-lifted on to a chair and a glass of Coca-Cola pushed into my hand. I drank some, then looked at the man who had ordered it. He hadn't taken part in the fight. I figured from the way everyone did as he said that he was the boss.

'You did all right, kid,' he said. 'That was a good fight you put up. You've got heart. The kid's got heart.'

The other guys nodded and smiled. I had been through an initiation ceremony, and I'd passed. I was in the gang now, one of their own, and from now on I was guaranteed their protection. I was too young to be a proper gang member, but I started hanging out with them after school and I'd do errands for them – I became what was known as a runner.

I'd taken the first steps into the whirlwind of trouble that starts with little misdemeanours and leads to serious crime.

There were often fights between rival gangs. It didn't take much provocation. All it needed was for one gang to come across another in the streets – maybe suspect them of trying to muscle in on their territory – and just one word would be enough. Even though I wasn't a fully fledged gang member and it wasn't in my nature to be violent, I had no choice but to join in. All the time I knew that what I was doing was wrong, but my life was once again controlled by fear. I didn't want to be in the gang but I didn't want to be outside it, either.

So I put on my street-wise face to hide the fear I felt inside, and I tried to live up to the image I wanted to create.

I was strutting down the street one day, about thirteen years old at this time, when a car pulled up alongside me. The driver leaned over, opened the door, and said to me, 'Get in.'

I hesitated. I knew he was a cop even though it was an unmarked car, and I didn't want anyone to see me being too helpful to the cops.

'Get in,' he said again.

I knew I didn't really have a choice, so I climbed into the passenger seat, closed the door and waited for him to speak. We drove down 148th Street, down St Anne's Avenue. There are maybe two thousand people living on each of these streets, and most have dead-end jobs, eking a living without opportunity or hope for a different future. For a while we sat silently and then, at last, he spoke.

'You know, don't you,' he said, 'that if you carry on the way you're going, you will be in serious trouble in a couple of years' time?'

'So what would you like me to do,' I asked, 'in this place? There's nothing, no choice but the streets.'

'There is an alternative. You could channel your energy in a different direction.'

'Whad'ya mean?'

'You like to fight in the streets, yeah?'

I nodded.

'Then why don't you fight in a boxing ring?'

I looked at him. He seemed an okay sort of guy but I wasn't sure why he was interested in me. I wasn't happy with the way my life was going but I didn't like being told what to do by a policeman. I thought about it for a minute, then I said, 'Okay, I'll go box in a ring . . . if I can box you.'

'You wanna box me?' he laughed.

'Yeah.'

The cop looked me up and down, then he nodded.

'Okay, Friday night we'll go down to the CYO hall.'

The Catholic Youth Organisation ran boxing clubs and

gyms across the city, so that Friday evening I made my way to Holy Cross Church in the Bronx. I stripped down to my shorts and put on the gloves they gave me to wear. The gloves were so heavy I could barely lift my arms, but I was ready. I'd made my plans. Whatever it took, I was going to make sure I won. If I couldn't knock him down fair and square, I'd kick him or do whatever I had to.

I climbed into the ring. My opponent followed me.

'Hi, Mikey, you all right?'

'Yeah, I'm fine. Now are we going to do this or what?'

The bell rang and I started dodging around him, throwing punches. Thirty seconds into the round, BOOM! The next thing I remember is opening my eyes and looking up from the floor of the boxing ring at the fluorescent light dangling from the ceiling. Thank God he didn't give me a full punch, just a short pop. The cop was standing over me, smiling.

'You all right, Mikey?' he asked.

I sat up and shook my head, trying to clear it.

'Yeah, I think so. What happened?'

The cop gave me a quick grin, then helped me up.

'Come on, let's get changed, we can talk out of the ring.'

There must have been two hundred people there for the regular Friday night fights and they were all watching us. I felt stupid and embarrassed, but in spite of that I couldn't help liking the guy. I could see that he cared.

His name was Jerry, and he was with the neighbourhood PAL – one of the community policemen from the Police Athletic League, whose job it was to encourage youngsters off the streets into sport.

'Why don't you come and box in the ring?' he said. 'You're good, and you could be very good if you had some proper training. We could work out together.'

I knew in my heart that I was headed for trouble if I stayed on the streets, plus I enjoyed sport of all kinds, so I jumped at the opportunity. With Jerry's help I started taking my boxing seriously. I trained in Joey Archer's Club. He was the middleweight champion of the world and I got to meet many people involved in all levels of the sport. I enjoyed boxing, but more than that I loved the workout, liked the people I was mixing with, and Jerry was like a big brother to me. Before I met him I was headed down a dead-end street; he pointed me in a different direction. At the time, I was just grateful for that; I had no idea then how the memory of him and how he encouraged me was to help determine my career and affect my whole life. Meeting Jerry was the first miracle.

Meanwhile I was getting to be a good boxer and I was starting to believe in myself. I had always suffered with low self-esteem – it's a problem for many people in the ghetto, where poverty has a way of bringing people down and keeping them there – but through the boxing, something I was able to do well, I was beginning to see that I did have some worth.

I wasn't really part of the gang any more and now, because I was fighting in the ring, I could distance myself from them. Boxing was a tough sport and boxers were highly thought of – the guys in the neighbourhood were proud of me. Gang members would often come and watch me fight. Sometimes I'd see the guys hanging out on street corners and I'd stop and talk to them, but I was always going training or on my way to a boxing match. I usually had a good excuse for not getting involved when they told me about fights.

Except one particular night. On my way home from training, I bumped into a couple of the guys I knew from the gang. They told me there was going to be a big fight on the streets that night. They were taking on another gang, old bitter rivals.

'Why don't you come, Mikey?'

'Yeah, we could do with a fighter like you on our side.'

I hesitated, then I said, 'Guys, I wish I could help you, but I've been training all evening, and I've got stuff to do now. I've gotta get back.'

'Hey, Mikey, this is for the honour of the gang. Aren't you part of our gang any more?'

His eyes narrowed as he spoke and they both stepped closer to me. A ripple of fear ran down my back. I didn't want to be singled out, to be seen as different, but I knew I had to dissociate myself from these guys. I'd managed to avoid any serious trouble up till now, but if I stayed with them it was only a matter of time. I had to make a decision.

'No, I'm not part of your gang any more,' I told them, and I immediately felt as if I'd been released from a tremendous pressure.

That night a man was clubbed to death with baseball bats. Some of the people I knew, guys I'd hung around with, wound up spending ten years in prison, and I could so easily have been with them. Everything could have been lost in one night, but I believe that God had his hand on me even then, and I thank him for that.

Things had changed for me since I had taken up boxing. Life was still tough, I was still living in the same neighbourhood in the same conditions, but I was enjoying life more. But even though things had improved for me, I still hurt for my friends, who'd been injured or sent to prison. I knew these guys well, knew their thoughts and fears – I was once one of them.

I was glad that I had found a way out through boxing, but I couldn't get away completely. I lived in the same apartment building as some of the guys. We'd pass each other on the stairs. Others lived on my block. When I went to school, they were there. There was tremendous peer pressure on kids to join. It's not easy to say no. I didn't want to get caught up again so I played hookey, staying away from school. I always seemed to be hiding, even from my own generation. I was trapped in my environment, and there was no way out. My folks couldn't afford to move. Long Island, with its wealthy residents with big houses and real gardens with grass, was only a few miles from the Bronx, but it might as well have been a million miles away.

But in spite of everything my life had gotten a lot better. As well as boxing, which I enjoyed, I was a good ball player. I had a strong throwing arm and I could catch a ball; I was a real good hitter and a fast runner. I was good enough to try out for the New York Yankees baseball team. Everything was going great for me. I was starting to feel good about myself and my future.

One Sunday afternoon, when I was about seventeen and a half, my family were sitting round the kitchen table in our apartment. My mom and dad, my sister Laura, Tommy, my twin, and my grandmother and grandfather were all there, when my older brother Johnny came in. He was home on leave from the army. The draft was in effect in the States in those days, and Johnny had been serving with his unit in Korea.

'Hi, Johnny, how's it going?' my dad asked.

'Good, Dad, it's going good, but I've got some orders I don't understand.'

He brought a letter out of his pocket and put it on the kitchen table.

'It says I'm going to Vi-et-nam. Did you ever hear of that?'

We all shook our heads. My dad said, 'Get out the atlas, Mike, we'll look it up, find out where our boy's going.'

We eventually found it, a little country on the other side of the world.

'What they sending you there for, Johnny?' my grandmother asked.

'Beats me, Grandma.'

No one thought any more about it. My family were proud to have a son serving his country, and whether he was in Korea or some place called Vietnam didn't make much difference to us – they were both a long way away.

While Johnny went off to Vietnam, my life carried on as usual. I had a big fight coming up just before Christmas 1964.

I was eighteen years old, and if I won this one I would move up a level from the sand-lot boxing I was doing at the time. It was an important fight and I was training hard, spending every spare minute at the gym, preparing myself physically and mentally. I came home one night after training and my mom was waiting for me. As soon as I came through the door, she shoved an envelope into my hand.

'This letter came for you, Mikey,' she said.

I took it from her. The envelope had an official stamp on it. I opened the letter and read it.

'What's it say, Mikey?' my mom asked anxiously. I think she had already guessed what was in the letter.

'It's my draft papers, Mom. It says I'm gonna be in the army.'

Chapter 3

With the arrival of my draft notice (call-up papers) all my fears and anxieties returned and a deep depression settled on me. I had thought that life was getting better for me. I had worked so hard to avoid the Bronx gang scene, done my best to keep out of trouble, and now it seemed that everything was going wrong again.

The war in Vietnam was escalating fast. Both Johnny and Tommy, my twin, were already out there – Johnny in the Marines and Tommy in the 101st Airborne Division – but none of my family really understood why they were there or what it was all about. My parents were proud that their sons were doing their duty, and it didn't occur to them to question why their boys had to go to a foreign country and fight in a strange war. As the children of émigrés, my parents still believed that the country was doing them a favour by taking them in.

But when my papers arrived, my mom decided enough was enough. She wrote to her Congressman and said she already had two sons risking their lives for their country and she couldn't bear the thought of possibly losing all three. He must have been sympathetic, because instead of being sent overseas

I spent my service time in Fort Jackson, South Carolina.

As it happened, my brothers both survived the war but they came home as changed men. Johnny suffered serious physical injury and now, more than thirty years later, is still heavily disabled. Tommy's outfit had been short of men; he had to do more than his normal tour of duty and, as a result, he had many serious problems. The first time I saw him, when I came home on leave and he was in bad shape, I couldn't believe it – he wasn't the same twin brother any more. In the years that followed, Tommy would have some severe relapses, and even today he is scarred by his experience.

My brothers' lives, and the lives of thousands like them, were damaged by that far-off war, and many families were torn apart. Great numbers of Vietnam veterans, who deserved to be treated as heroes, came home instead to a country that had no place for them, to a land that was changing rapidly. America in the late 1960s was in the throes of revolution: the Beatles and pop invaded the music scene, the hippie movement of love and peace started, and drug-taking was becoming commonplace.

But for me, at least, some things never changed. My fear of dying and of hell was as real as ever. I had started going to confession again sometimes and I liked the way I felt holy when I came out of church. I was never suicidal, I would never have taken my own life, but there were times when I would have been grateful if a car had come around the corner, at just the right moment as I left the church, and knocked me down, securing me a place in heaven instead of certain hell.

Just before Christmas 1966, I was coming up to the end of my service time and I was home on leave when I bumped into my old friend Joey in the street.

'Mikey!'

'Joey!'

We hugged and kissed each other on both cheeks Italian-style. It had been a long time since we'd last met.

'How you doing, Mikey?'

'I'm doing good, Joey, how about you? How's life in the Marine Corps?'

'Aah,' he flicked his head. 'It's all right. Hey, you heard about the party tonight?'

'Party, what party?'

'Seems like everybody from our old crowd is getting together.'

My spirits were low and I figured a party would cheer me up a little. I arranged to meet Joey at the hall later.

'And don't forget to wear your uniform,' he shouted as we separated.

I was excited. I hadn't see my old friends in some time and I was looking forward to getting together with them and finding out all their news.

That evening, I bathed and dressed carefully. I brushed down my uniform – I was still proud of it, proud to be serving my country – and then I headed off for the hall where the party was taking place. I pushed open the door and walked in. The place was packed with gals and guys in uniforms of all kinds. There was an excitement and buzz in the air. Joey spotted me straight away and shouted, 'Mikey, over here. Hey, guys, look, it's Mikey Di!'

Suddenly I was surrounded by old friends, all hugging and kissing me. We exchanged news: I heard about who'd been wounded and who hadn't made it back from the war, and I told them what I'd been doing. Then I put up my hand to interrupt them.

'Guys, I'm just gonna get myself a drink – it's thirsty work, all this talking.'

I turned round and was about to make my way to the bar when I stopped. A girl was sitting on a chair against the wall at the opposite side of the hall. She was wearing a miniskirt and a white blouse with a red bow tie. She turned and smiled as she said something to her friend, and the words of the old song came back to me – 'in Dublin's fair city, where the girls are so pretty'. She had that sort of an 'Irish' face.

'Oh boy,' I said to myself, 'I have gotta ask that girl to dance.'

Forgetting the drink, I started to make my way across the dance floor. I knew I had to ask this girl to dance before someone else got there first.

'Mikey, how you doing, man?'

Charlie, my old softball buddy, grabbed me by the shoulders and kissed me. He was in the Marines now.

'I'm doing fine, Charlie. How you doing?'

I listened to him as he filled me in on all his news, all the time watching, over his shoulder, the girl still sitting at the edge of the dance floor. Eventually I said, 'Charlie, can I talk to you later? There's something I gotta do right now.'

'Sure, Mikey, I'll catch you later.'

I slapped him on the shoulder and hurriedly carried on across the dance floor – only to be stopped again and again by guys and gals I hadn't seen for a long time. I was sure someone else would get to her first, but finally I found myself near her chair. Now I hesitated. What if she said no? I was still low on self-esteem and I didn't want to be rejected. But something in me knew that if something good was going to happen, it was going to happen here.

'Excuse me,' I said. 'Would you like to dance?'

She looked up right into my face.

'Sure.'

Wow! I couldn't believe that she'd said yes. I figured I must be the luckiest man in the place that night. The band was playing a slow dance and I led her on to the floor and put my arm around her waist.

'In the still of the night, I held you, held you tight, cos I loved you, loved you.' The words danced in the air. I could feel a new hope, a sense that something in this girl was going to be

24

special. In a world that was messed up, she was pretty and calm, she was what I needed.

There was an unwritten law in the Bronx dance hall: if a girl agreed to sit down with you, it meant that she would stay with you for the evening; if she wasn't that interested in you and wanted to dance with other guys, she wouldn't sit down; and if she said yes and then another guy asked her to dance, the boys would take him outside and recorrect his thinking. That's just the way it was in the Bronx. It was all understood.

The song was coming to an end and I knew I had to ask this girl to sit down with me, but again I was scared of rejection. Only now it was even worse, because I'd held her in my arms for ten minutes, and the thought of it being all over was too much. The music ended. I had to do it.

'Would you like to sit with me?'

'Sure.'

For the second time that evening I couldn't believe my luck. I stood and grinned at her, not moving.

'Shall we sit down then?' she asked, after a few minutes.

'Sure,' I said, still not moving.

'There are some empty chairs over there,' she said. 'Shall we sit there?'

'Oh, yeah, sure,' I said and started to lead the way, thinking, 'Pull yourself together, Mikey, she'll think you're a real jerk at this rate.'

We spent the rest of the evening dancing and talking and getting to know each other. Her name was Ann and her family had come over to New York City from Ireland. Every time I looked at her, she seemed to get prettier. At the end of the evening, I took her home in my '57 Chevy, a candy-apple red convertible, and asked her if I could see her again. Then I asked Ann's parents if I could take their daughter out. That was the way it was done then. The sexual revolution hadn't yet happened.

Three months later, Ann's family decided to go back to Ireland. They had realised that America wasn't the place for them. Ann and I were still seeing each other and were serious about each other, so we got engaged, and on 4th May 1968 we were married in Holy Cross Catholic Church.

We got an apartment in the Soundview Avenue area of the Bronx. In the kitchen we had a table with four milk crates around it; the living room was so empty that if you shouted 'yo', it shouted back at you; and in the bedroom we had a box spring and mattress. We might have been short on material goods, but we were in love and we were happy.

Meeting Ann was my second miracle.

By now I was out of the army, and Ann and I were both working in menial jobs. Every Friday night we'd pool our wages and put money aside for all the bills: the food and the heating, and even our subway fares. By the time we'd budgeted our money we were left with $6, which paid for our pizza and our Friday night out.

I only earned the minimum wage but it was the best I could hope for. I'd spent so much time playing hookey from school I didn't have a high school diploma, and it was impossible to get any sort of decent job without that vital piece of paper.

One night Ann came into the apartment and gave me a brochure.

'I picked it up at the subway station,' she said. 'Why don't you apply for it?'

It was a New York Police Department recruitment brochure.

I shook my head. 'Poor Annie,' I thought, 'she's been in the Bronx too long, it's affecting her mind.' I said, 'I can't apply, Ann, you need a diploma before they'll even let you take the test, and you know I haven't got any education.'

'Okay, then get a diploma.'

'How can I get a diploma? I'm not a kid in school any more.'

'You can go back to night school and get one.'

'I can't do that, Ann.'

I still had no confidence in my abilities and I really believed I wasn't smart enough to get a diploma, but Ann had other ideas. She encouraged me to enrol, helped me, made sure I did all the homework, and was the first to kiss and congratulate me when I got my diploma. But she wasn't going to let me rest up.

'Good,' she said, 'now you can try the NYPD test.'

'Oh, Ann, I don't know.'

I still wasn't sure if I wanted to be a policeman, but then I thought of Jerry, the community policeman who'd helped me off the streets into the ring. If it hadn't been for him my life could have been very different – in fact I would probably have been dead by now. Maybe it would be possible for me to help others in the same way.

'Do you think I could do it, Ann?'

'Course you can, Mike, I know you can.'

I started studying again. We got out books of past questions from the police exams and every evening we would go through them. Ann would test me till she was certain I knew the answers. She'd try and fool me by swapping questions around and asking them in different ways, and she wouldn't let me rest until she was happy.

'Aw, Ann, I'm exhausted. Can't we stop for tonight?'

'Not yet, Mike, there's too much to learn. You can have just a short break and then we'll do some more.'

My Annie was a hard taskmaster.

At last the day of the test came. Ann came with me to the George Washington High School where I was to take the test, and she waited outside for the whole time while I did the written test. When I came out, she ran up to me.

'How'd you do, Mikey?'

'I don't know, Ann, some good, some bad. The first question: no problem. The second: I don't think there's a problem. The third: eeny, meeny, miny, mo.'

I wasn't too hopeful of my chances. Out of the 50,000 who were taking the test, only 4,000 would be accepted. The pass mark was 80 per cent.

'Lots of those guys doing the test will be smarter than me,' I said. 'How'm I gonna get through?'

'Mikey, listen to me,' Ann said. 'Even if you don't make it, you tried. That's what matters.'

Now I had my high school diploma, I was able to apply for other jobs as well. Over the weeks I took tests for the Post Office and the subway and anything else Ann could find. Then one night, about six weeks after I sat the NYPD test, I got home from work to find Ann at the kitchen sink. As I came through the door, she spun round to face me, her face alight.

'Guess what?' she said.

'What?'

'You passed!'

I looked at her blankly.

'Passed what?'

'The NYPD test.'

'What? I passed?'

'You did!'

'Wha'd I get?'

'You got 92.'

'A what?'

'You got 92 out of 100.'

'I got 92 per cent! Wow!'

It finally sank in, and I grabbed Ann and hugged her. We danced around the kitchen, then I said, 'Get your coat, we gotta celebrate.'

We rushed out of the apartment and down the stairs two at a time. Holding hands we ran outside into the road, down to the subway. We got on to the train and off at the next stop, 125th Street, then back up to the road and into Anthony's Pizza Shop in Harlem. We were going to have a grand celebration.

We sat in the shop, eating our pizza, still hardly able to believe it. This wasn't just a better job, with more money. I'd get benefits too. Neither of us got benefits – you had to have blood coming out of you before you'd get to a doctor, and if you had flu you still went to work – you couldn't afford to stay home.

'We can have some orange curtains for the kitchen. I've seen some I like,' Ann said, 'and some of those orange canisters for coffee and sugar.'

We were both so excited, talking of our plans for the future, when suddenly Ann started to cry. I reached out for her hand.

'What's the matter, babe?'

'This is our chance, Mike, don't you see, our chance to get out of the ghetto for good.'

I looked at her and realised she was right. This was the opportunity of our lives. Maybe our children wouldn't have to grow up the way we did.

Passing the test was just the first step to becoming a policeman. The next step was four months' training in the police academy, the equivalent of the army's West Point. A new world opened up for me there. I was now with guys from all over New York. I got to know guys who I would work with for many years, and I made a lot of good friends. Because we lined up for drill in alphabetical order I got to know best the guys who had names that started with letters early in the alphabet! I stood next to Shamus Dillon: he became my friend and partner for a number of years. He was from Scotland so we called him – you've guessed it – Scotty.

New recruits had to learn everything from penal law to first aid, and we had to be in top physical condition. I ran five to ten miles a day on my own and another five in the academy. At the end of the course we had to sit four exams and a physical fitness test, and pass them all. Failing just one would mean you flunked out of the academy.

It wasn't long before all my old fears returned yet again. What if I failed? I had the chance now of a job, a career that would give me security for my family. This was just in my sights. To fail now, knowing what I was losing, would be even worse. Ann once again encouraged me.

'You can do it, Mike. You didn't think you'd get this far, but you have. You can do it and I'll help you all I can.'

She was as good as her word, and night after night we sat up till midnight going over the books, Ann asking me questions until I got them right. Sometimes we'd argue.

'I can't take any more, Ann, leave me alone!'

'Quiet up and get on with it, Mike, you're going to do this.'

By the end of the six months I was in top physical and mental shape, and I passed all the police exams. It was a great feeling, but somewhere deep inside me a fear still gnawed at me. I was in poor shape spiritually. Even though I didn't go to church any more, I still knew in my heart that I was destined for hell. I had broken many of the rules that my religion had taught me, and I was condemned: that knowledge stayed with me all the time, even if I kept it buried below the surface.

On graduation day my whole family came to the ceremony to watch. My family had a special place in their hearts for policemen, and to have a son graduate from the police academy was a great honour.

After the ceremony my dad came up to me and hugged me and kissed me. Then he held me at arm's length.

'Mike, I'm so proud of you.'

'I know you are, Pop.'

He pulled me close and hugged me again, then stepped back and was about to move away when he changed his mind. He caught my shoulders and was going to draw me in again when I said, 'Whoa, Pop, everybody's looking.' People all around us were watching, and smiling because they understood. My dad looked around and laughed and slapped me on the shoulders instead. We were a tough little family, but we'd gone through a lot of heartbreak over what Vietnam had done to us. This day meant a lot to us all.

We paraded down the streets, thousands of new graduates in full uniform with wives or girlfriends proudly by our sides. Ann walked with me holding my hand, laughing and smiling with pride. We were both so happy, looking forward to a new future.

Before the ceremony began, all the new cops were given their first assignment. I joined the crowd in the room, waiting for an envelope with my name on it to be put into my white-gloved hands. I saw Scotty sitting on a bench with his envelope in his hand, and I went over and sat next to him. We both opened our letters and read silently.

'What you got, Scotty?' I asked.

He didn't say anything but showed me his letter. I looked at it, then showed him mine. We had the same assignment – Harlem.

'Oh, boy,' we groaned together.

Chapter 4

'Officer DiSanza reporting for duty, sir!'

As a young rookie fresh out of police academy, I stood smartly to attention before the white-haired Irish desk sergeant. It was just before midnight on the first night of my first tour of duty in my new precinct, and I was following to the letter the instructions I had been taught. This was how you did it, according to the manual and the instructors; this was how you reported for duty. You presented yourself to the desk sergeant or lieutenant and requested your assignment.

The desk sergeant on duty on this particular night seemed unaware of these rules. Through glasses perched on the end of his nose he continued to study the papers on the desk, ignoring me standing in front of him.

After a few minutes, I tried again, slightly louder this time, 'Officer DiSanza reporting for duty, sir!'

The sergeant slowly raised his head and cast a casual glance at me.

'So?' he spat out, before resuming his reading.

This wasn't what I had been expecting. This wasn't how the desk sergeant was supposed to react. I looked around; there was no one else I could ask. So I tried again.

'Officer DiSanza reporting for duty and needing a locker for his equipment, sir.'

The sergeant sighed deeply and looked wearily at the eager young rookie standing to attention before him. 'Hey, you wanna locker, right? Lockers are downstairs. Go get yourself a locker and leave me alone.'

He growled the words, clearly resenting the breath he had to waste, and returned to his reading.

I looked around the room again. There were a number of unmarked doors, any one of which could have led downstairs – or anywhere else for that matter. I didn't want to walk into the wrong room, maybe even the captain's office, and make a fool of myself on my first tour. There were no clues to help me so I figured I'd have to choose one and hope it was the right one.

Just then a door at the side of the desk opened and a burly patrolman came out through it. He stood there, smoking his cigar, his shirt stretched over his belly and his gun belt hanging loosely round his backside. Everything about him said 'veteran'.

'Hey, kid, don't worry about him,' he said, nodding in the direction of the sergeant. 'He's been around here a little too long.'

'Pah,' the sergeant grunted without lifting his eyes from his papers.

'Come on, I'll show you round.'

As we made our way downstairs, the veteran cop introduced himself.

'I'm Rocky,' he said. 'Don't worry, you'll soon get used to this place. We're not all as bad as him.'

In the dusty spider's web that was the basement locker room, Rocky pointed to an empty locker.

'Okay, kid, this is your locker. Put your stuff in there, get into uniform, come out and I'll take care of you.'

Then he went, leaving me to change.

I undressed, put on my uniform, stowed my duffel bag and street clothes in my locker, and viewed myself in the mirror. There, reflected back at me and looking as shiny as the presidential limousine from the historic badge on my hat to my highly polished shoes, was one of the newest members of New York Police District 2. As I stood there, I remembered my graduation ceremony and the way my father had hugged and kissed me, not once but twice, pride oozing from every pore. Ann didn't need to tell me how delighted she and all my family were that I was getting a chance to better myself – I had seen it in the excitement in their faces. They all knew this was mine and Ann's opportunity, maybe only chance, to escape from the ghetto.

I straightened my cap, tightened my gun belt and made my way back up to the desk to look for Rocky. He wasn't there. There was no sign of anyone except the sergeant, still engrossed in his papers. There was no other choice but . . .

'Sergeant, this is Officer DiSanza requesting to know his assignment, sir!'

'You still here? Right, let's settle this now. You wanna know your assignment, right?'

He grabbed the roll call.

'What's your name?'

'Officer DiSanza, sir.'

'DiSanza, DiSanza.' He scanned the roll call. 'You got 110th Street in Spanish Harlem. You got that? You sure you got that, are you?'

'Yes, Sergeant.'

At that point, I should have saluted, turned and headed for the door, but with a sinking heart I realised I still had a problem. I stayed standing smartly to attention before the desk. The sergeant was watching, drumming his fingers on the desk, waiting for me to go. Finally he snapped.

'Wassa matter now? Whadya want now?'

'How do I get to 110th Street, sir?'

The sergeant slammed down the roll call, levered himself out of his chair and made his way to the front door, with me in close pursuit.

'You wanna know where 110th Street is? You know where this is, do you? This is 125th Street. You got that?'

'Yes, sergeant.'

'Tell me where you are, boy.'

'125th Street, Sergeant.'

'Right, you walk fifteen blocks south – watch my fingers – south, you got that, south? And if you make it, you're on 110th Street.'

With that, he turned and walked back into the building, leaving me alone on the steps wondering what on earth I was doing there.

Before leaving police academy, all of us new recruits had often discussed possible assignments and locations. One thing we were all agreed upon was that nobody wanted Harlem. Its reputation was fearsome. The ghettos stretched for miles; at any time of day or night, the streets were full of all types of people. On every corner, gangs hung out waiting for trouble, which came with the certainty of night following day. It was not a good place to be a cop.

Setting off down the street, I followed the sergeant's instructions to 'go south for fifteen blocks'. As I walked, I could hear low whistling voices coming out of the shadows on all sides: 'We see you, rookie', 'You're new round here, boy', 'Don't you look good in your nice new uniform, boy', 'We're gonna get you, rookie.'

Smaassh. A brick flew through the darkness and hit a parked car just in front of me.

'Somebody call a cop . . .' the words died in my mouth as I remembered, with a sinking heart, that *I* was a cop. A new young cop, riddled with fear, battling with the impulse to turn and run, but a cop all the same.

Well, I might be a rookie but I had sense enough to realise that there was no point in trying to find the brick-thrower – there were hundreds of people in the shadows – so I continued to make my way to my new beat. Trying to walk tall, fighting my nervousness, I walked the dark streets, the taunting cries ringing in my head, until eventually I made it to 110th Street, where all seemed quiet.

But this was Spanish Harlem, New York, and things didn't stay quiet for long. With the bars open until 4 a.m., it was almost inevitable that among the drinking hordes trouble would arise. This particular night it was a stabbing. As I walked my beat, I saw the light from a street lamp reflect off a blade as one man pulled a knife on another.

I saw the blade and I froze. But then a voice in my head said, 'You're a cop – do something!'

I had to draw on all my inner resources as I ran towards the two perpetrators. The crowds saw me coming, and right away they formed a human blockade around the fighters. This was their world, their people – they didn't want a cop interfering.

'Excuse me, let me through please, excuse me.'

'Hey, the cop wants to get through. Shall we let the nice policeman through?'

The taunting crowds laughed in my face. I was in their territory, with its own rules and regulations. Its inhabitants weren't going to accept interference from anyone, least of all a rookie cop.

I struggled to assert my authority, but it was an uneven battle and all I could do was wrestle helplessly at the edge of the crowd, unable to make any headway, feeling useless.

Whoou, whoou, whoou.

The wailing siren of a fast-approaching police car sounded sweeter to my ears than the Drifters ever had.

The car screeched to a halt beside the curb. Cops leapt out

and charged into the crowd. They didn't mess around. Pushing people aside, they cuffed anyone who resisted. Within minutes, the crowd had dispersed, troublemakers were arrested and relative peace was restored.

Then they spoke to me.

'We heard on the radio about a knife fight and guessed you'd need some help. This your first assignment?'

'Yeah, my first night.'

'Who's your sarge?'

When I told them, they laughed sympathetically.

'Welcome to Harlem. We're here to help you. We would have come down to say hello but it's been a busy night.'

And so my career in the police department was well and truly under way. It had been a first night in which I learned a lot.

I'd seen the way the guys handled trouble. They used the necessary force to bring everything under control, but no one got badly injured. I realised then that if you hesitate, you're in trouble. This was very serious stuff.

Over the years, stabbings, murders, riots, muggings and all sorts of crime formed part of my daily life, but I never said 'excuse me' again.

A month or so later I answered another call, this time on the streets of Manhattan. The first thing I saw when I got there was a cop, slumped in the gutter in a pool of his own blood. A man, who I guessed was his assailant, was standing over him, holding in his hands a nightstick. A short distance away I could see several other police officers standing motionless. I was puzzled.

Here was this guy, a fellow officer, who was obviously badly injured, and no one was doing anything to help him. Nobody was trying to apprehend his attacker, they were all just standing around. I couldn't understand it.

A few seconds later it all became clear. The assailant took a few stumbling steps and fell to the ground. I realised then that a shot must have been fired before I arrived on the scene. The man had been wounded but it had taken a short while for the bullet to take its full effect.

It was the first time I'd seen a cop injured in the line of duty. It brought home to me the very real possibility of being seriously wounded while doing my job. As I waited for the ambulance to come for the injured man, I realised that, in the years to come, it was likely that I was going to be involved in many situations where my life would be on the line.

It's not unusual for police officers to find themselves in life and death situations where decisions have to be made instantly, where there is no time for careful considered planning. As police cadets in the academy we were taught that our duty was to prevent injury to others and to ourselves.

Most police action is, and has to be, reaction, and situations that demanded immediate reaction happened frequently.

One evening I was called to a knife fight on a subway train. When I arrived on the scene, the subway car was in chaos. The noise of the train whistle was drowned out by the screams and cries of people panicking and trying to distance themselves from the trouble. I didn't bother with 'excuse me' this time, I just pushed my way against the flow through the crowds until I could see the two men involved in the incident. As I got closer, the attacker spotted me and lunged at me in a frenzy of fury.

I saw the blade coming towards my face and I instinctively put up my hands to protect myself. As I did so, the blade caught me across the palm of my hand, making a deep gash between my thumb and first finger. Blood started pouring from the wound. I had seconds in which to make a vital decision: should I go for my gun? The carriage was full of late-night revellers, and if it came to a shoot-out it was possible that an innocent bystander might be hurt. There was also the danger that the attacker or, if he were not alone, one of his friends, could grab the gun, making the situation worse. The decision was made – I couldn't use my gun. Instead, I had to disarm and restrain the man with physical force. The two of us struggled in an uneven-looking fight: the attacker still had the knife and I was bleeding heavily. The original victim and the passengers now felt safe because a cop was on the scene, and they stood and watched as we wrestled this way and that, each of us trying to get the upper hand.

The NYPD has to ensure that the men it sends out on to the streets are ready to cope with all situations, and I was in good shape, strong and well-trained in self-defence. In a one-to-one situation it was unlikely that I would be outmanoeuvred. And so it proved to be.

I was soon able to disarm my attacker and take control of the fight. I forced the man on to the floor, twisted his arms back and cuffed him. Then I took a deep breath, and allowed myself to relax a little. I stood up, pulled the man to his feet and dragged him to the doors just as the train pulled into the next stop. The district had been alerted and there were officers waiting on the platform for us.

In the course of the incident, decisions were made so fast and action taken so quickly that there was no time for me to be scared or doubtful, but later, as I sat in the hospital waiting for the stitches I needed in my hand, my emotions welled up. I thought, 'Three months down, twenty years to go. How will I ever last?'

In an effort to save money, the NYPD had cut back the number of their patrolmen, which meant that cops often had to do tours of duty alone rather than with a partner.

Every time a New York police officer sets out on his beat, especially if it covers areas like the South Bronx and Harlem, he knows it's quite likely that he's going to have to tackle incidences of violence, depravity and cruelty. If you're going to face these issues every day, you have to find a way of dealing with them. Many cops choose to bury their emotions.

I wasn't able to discuss or even admit to the way I was feeling with anyone, and my tangled emotions fermented inside me. Fear that had been simmering since my youth grew in power, bringing with it the associated problems of depression and anxiety.

While on patrol one day in Manhattan, I noticed some graffiti painted on the wall of a bank. It said, 'God is dead, signed Chico.' Next to it, someone else had written, 'Chico is dead, signed God.'

The graffiti reminded me of the existence of God, but then when I was on patrol, witnessing all kinds of evil, I used to ask myself, 'Where is God in this? How can there be a God in New York City?'

As well as evil, I saw many hurting people. New York, like many other cities, had and still has a high percentage of homeless people, who live on the streets or the subways and pass their time wandering around aimlessly or huddled over gratings on the pavements, grateful, especially in the bitterly cold winters, for the warm air coming from the electricity generators of buildings. The homeless of New York at that time included a lot of Vietnam veterans who had returned home to a country that didn't seem to appreciate what they'd done. Most were traumatised by their experiences of war, and many had acquired a drinking problem or drug habit while fighting in their country's army.

Also among the homeless were women who had been thrown out by their menfolk and who had nowhere to go. They too walked the streets, with their belongings in a shopping bag and maybe a child in tow. The sight of all this suffering caused me tremendous pain and became a burden I always carried with me.

But I had no idea how to help them. The best I could do was find them a bed for a night – or a week if they were lucky.

Within six months of graduating from the police academy, I was a changed man. I was becoming cold-hearted. I could understand why the sergeant on my first day couldn't care less, why so many cops on the South Bronx looked miserable, why so many cops died young. It seemed the only way to endure the job was to become hard, and I was rapidly going down that road.

My marriage came under pressure. I never talked about my work at home or told Ann how I was feeling, but she bore the brunt of my deepening depression. She couldn't help but notice the change in me. I wasn't the same warm, fun-to-be-with man she had married.

My physical health was also deteriorating; I suffered from high blood pressure attacks and had frequent nosebleeds.

I needed help; part of me acknowledged that. But I was still on probation, and I was well aware that any sign of mental or physical illness would get me removed from duty and out of the force. This was more than a job, this was my escape route from the ghetto. I couldn't go off sick and there was no one I could talk to. I was terrified I'd lose my job, the job I'd worked so hard for, the job that had so thrilled my family.

When you live in the ghetto all your life and you get a job which gives you a chance to get out, you're not too ready to give up that job, no matter what pressures come against you. I told myself, 'This is the best opportunity you'll ever have: don't let it get away.'

And anyway, I was a New York cop. New York cops were macho, tough guys who didn't break down. I had an outward image to maintain, a public face to put on with my uniform, to reassure the people on the street that I was the strong man on whom they could depend.

But inside I was crying, 'I'm hurting.'

On patrol one cold winter's night, I watched the wind whip up and scatter the garbage and debris. As I stood under the streetlights and saw the litter and dirt being thrown here and there, the bleakness of my situation was brought home to me.

The scene before me seemed to be a picture of my life. I was being tossed around by the black moods I was experiencing. I had no sun, no joy, no life. I was on the verge of a complete mental, physical and spiritual breakdown.

Chapter 5

The days and weeks began to merge under a cloud of blackness. Each tour of duty brought more and more horrific incidents for me to face and deal with. Working mostly nights, there were not many good calls. While most decent people in New York City were asleep in their beds, the streets came alive for those for whom darkness brought its own advantages.

One night, during a particularly violent tussle, I took a blow to my head. I finished my shift, but by the time I got home my head was aching badly and I had started vomiting. I was showing all the signs of concussion. Ann packed me off to bed and pleaded with me to report in sick.

'Mike, you're injured,' she said. 'You've got to go see a doctor.'

'I can't, Ann. I'm still on probation. You know what the department's like. If they think I'm not up to the job, they won't keep me on.'

'But you're not ill, you've been injured. They'll understand that.'

All Ann's pleading was in vain. I wasn't taking any chances; this was a job I couldn't afford to lose, too much depended on it. So in spite of feeling unwell I was going to report in as normal for my next shift.

The following day, still weak and dizzy and suffering from the effects of the blow, I was back on patrol in Harlem. I was standing on a corner in uniform when suddenly two caskets – coffins – appeared in front of me. I stopped, confused, then walked closer and looked in. Laid out in the caskets, dressed in their Sunday best, were my father and my mother.

Now I knew that my parents had been alive when I'd spoken to them only the day before, and if anything had happened to them I would have heard fast enough; word soon got round the neighbourhood. But my physical (and emotional and spiritual) state was such that I couldn't see the impossibility of the situation. I didn't realise that I was hallucinating the caskets. All my fevered brain was able to register was that my dearly loved mother and father were dead and they were lying in wooden boxes right in front of me. I was overcome with emotion and I dropped to one knee. A sharp pain shot through my head and blood started flowing from my nose and my mouth, but I was scarcely aware of it; all I knew was that I had to pray for the souls of my dead parents. That was important. From the recesses of my memory, religious practices I'd learned as a boy growing up in the Catholic Church came back to me. A jumble of words I'd forgotten I ever knew tumbled out of my mouth as I prayed for mercy on their souls.

Suddenly, through the mist of my confusion I felt my hand being gripped. I looked up. An elderly black woman was kneeling beside me.

'What's the matter, Officer?' she asked.

'My mother and father are dead.'

'I understand, officer, but Jesus is with you. Jesus loves you.' As she spoke, the bleeding stopped.

I clung on to her hand. I felt I was on the verge of death, and something in her touch made me hang on; I didn't want to let go.

The woman continued to talk gently to me. She told me about Jesus, the Son of God, who loved me, and she encouraged me to read the Bible when I felt well enough.

'Ask God to guide you,' she said.

She stayed with me until I felt strong enough to stand, then she helped me to my feet. I looked around. I had fallen directly in front of and below a fluorescent cross in the window of a storefront church. Beneath the cross, in bright lights, were the words, 'Jesus saves'.

By now my uniform was covered in my own blood, and I made my way unsteadily back to the precinct. I was forced to acknowledge at last that, if I were to continue to do my job properly, I needed some time to recover from my injury. I went home and took a few days off.

It was such a relief to get away from the horrors of my job for a while. A few days of rest and relaxation helped me to appreciate exactly what a serious effect the stress was having on me and my marriage. But even so, the facts remained the same: my job was a way out of the ghetto; I wouldn't get a better opportunity; and if I left the police department it wasn't only myself I'd be letting down but my whole family. I was in sombre mood as I considered my future, but then I remembered the words of the woman who had helped me in the street. 'Read the Bible,' she'd said.

Reading the Bible? This was a new idea to me. In the Catholic church I'd grown up in, ordinary people weren't encouraged to read the Bible. All I'd ever learned of God and Jesus had come through the priest. I thought again about the woman in the street, and made my decision. I looked around the apartment. I knew there had to be a Bible somewhere – every Italian home kept one – and I soon spotted it, on a lace doily on the end table. I walked over, picked it up and went back to sit at the kitchen table.

I looked at the big old book for a few minutes. I was still doubtful. Should I do this? What would the priest say?

Although I hadn't been in a church for many years, the rules were clearly imprinted on my brain.

But the woman had sounded so sure, so convinced that reading the Bible would help me, that it overcame my doubts, and I opened the book and turned to the beginning.

'Genius,' I read.

I read it again.

'Genius? What's that supposed to mean?'

It didn't make sense. I read on through the first few paragraphs, then I slammed the book shut impatiently. None of it made any sense.

Yet something kept nagging at me. I sat back in my chair and tried to remember. Memories floated in and out of my brain, until at last one particular incident settled there and took shape.

I must have been about thirteen or fourteen years old at the time, and walking in Times Square, 42nd Street. A man standing on an upturned milk crate had been speaking to the passers-by through the megaphone he carried in his hand. Suddenly he'd pointed at me.

'You!' he had shouted. 'When you get saved, read the Gospel of John.'

I had been horrified, flushed red with embarrassment, yet I couldn't move.

'Why me?' I'd thought. 'Why is this man picking me out in front of all these people?' But alongside the shame I couldn't help but feel a grudging respect and admiration for the speaker.

Now, sitting at the kitchen table eight years later, I recalled what the man had said.

Hesitantly I picked up the Bible again. I flicked through the pages until I came upon a painting of a bearded man in flowing robes carrying a sheep. Underneath the painting were the words, 'I am the Good Shepherd.'

I stared at the painting and a flicker of recognition dawned in me. 'And that's me,' I thought. 'I'm the sheep.'

I looked at the painting for a while, wondering what it all meant, before turning the page to discover 'The Gospel according to John'.

I was still unconvinced. How could I hope to make sense of a book if I started two-thirds of the way into it? It seemed stupid, but as I remembered the words of the street preacher I decided I had nothing to lose, and I began reading.

The Bible I was using was an old one, and the language was old-fashioned, with lots of 'thees' and 'thous'. It was difficult to understand, but I did my best until I reached chapter three, verse sixteen of the Gospel of John. I know now that this is one of the best-known verses in the Bible. It's a verse that you'll often see on sandwich boards and billboards at railway stations and on street corners, as well as outside church buildings. I read, 'For God so loved the world that he gave his only begotten son, Jesus Christ, that whosoever believed in him would not perish but have everlasting life.'

Again, I know now that these are words that have caused many people to take their first steps towards God, but my reaction was slightly different.

'Oh, no,' I thought, 'who wants to live for ever?'

All my life I'd lived alongside violence and poverty. If everlasting life meant enduring those conditions for ever, I didn't want it. I'd reached the point in my life when death looked good because it offered a way out.

But I read on. The next verse said, 'For God did not send Jesus to condemn you, but to save you.'

The words jumped off the page at me. 'For God did not send Jesus to condemn you, Mike, but to save you.'

For anyone growing up in the Bronx, condemnation was part of life. Most people believed that if you were born in the ghetto you must have done something real bad in a previous life. If you lived there, you had no future, you were condemned – it was as simple as that.

For me, all these negative feelings were reinforced by a Catholic upbringing that focused on wrongdoing and punishment. As far as I was concerned, I was destined for hell and there was nothing I could do about it. I had heard of Jesus, sure, but it was always as someone who was out to get me, not the sort of person anyone would want for a friend. But now here I was, reading that Jesus was sent not to condemn me, Mike, but to save me.

This was a radical turnaround. Was it possible that all my beliefs and the things I'd learned as a child were based on an alternative version of the truth? Maybe I'd got Jesus wrong. I was ready to acknowledge my need, and in a trembling voice I said, 'Jesus, whoever you are, help me.'

I put down the Bible and sat back in my chair. I felt as if a weight had been lifted off me. A peace that I'd never known before came over me and, with my head on the kitchen table, I fell into a deep sleep and dreamed a vivid dream.

In front of me I saw two huge wooden doors with a large iron bar across them. The bar slid back, the doors opened and I could hear screaming. Now, I'm a New York cop and I've heard some screaming in my time, but this was like nothing I'd ever heard. The screaming was coming from a gigantic pit. I couldn't see the bottom. It was black. I was walking towards the edge of the pit and I knew I was going down into that hole. I knew once you were in that pit, you never ever got out, no matter how hard you tried, and I knew I was going down and it was for ever. I was terrified. I was just starting to go down when a hand grabbed me and jerked me out. Next thing I knew I was outside the doors and they were closing. I heard a voice behind me say, 'You don't belong in there, you belong to me. You will do great exploits for me.' I just heard the voice, I didn't see a face, but I knew it was Jesus and I knew I was on my way, wherever I was going, and it was for ever.

I woke up suddenly from my dream. I was sweating and my heart was thumping. I had been through a near-death experience, and I'd been saved from the pit of hell. The prayer to Jesus I'd cried just before I'd fallen asleep had been answered.

I couldn't wait for Ann to get home from work that day. Although I'd made a point of never telling her of the horrific scenes I witnessed day by day, I realised that she must have been aware of a change in me, a change I had felt helpless to prevent. When she walked through the doorway that evening, I jumped up from my chair, ran across the room, and kissed her. The look of amazement on her face said it all. I beamed.

'Hi, honey.'

'Mike, what happened to you? You're glowing. You look so . . . peaceful.'

'Sit down, Ann, let me tell you.'

I told her all that had happened to me, beginning with my collapse in the street and ending with the dream.

'Jesus didn't come to condemn us, Ann, and I feel so good.'

'Well, whatever the reason, you look great.'

Nothing in my Catholic background had prepared me for an encounter with God like the one I'd experienced. In the weeks that followed, if anyone had asked me for an explanation of what had happened to me, I'd have been stuck for words. All I knew was that something great had happened and I wanted to share it with others. Every time I tried to talk to Ann about it, she made an excuse. She was busy or tired or about to go out. She made it clear that she wasn't interested. I was sad that she felt like that, but I hoped she'd come round if I gave her time.

Although Ann didn't seem interested, I was sure that there were others who would be, and I wanted to tell them but didn't know how to go about it. Then I remembered the man on the street with the megaphone and the way he'd tried to tell people about God, and it gave me an idea.

I borrowed a bullhorn – a police loudhailer – from the precinct and headed again for Spanish Harlem. Finding a good spot on the corner of 110th Street I lifted the bullhorn to my mouth. As I prepared to speak, I looked around at the crowds of people rushing past, hurrying to work or shopping or going home. Everyone had somewhere to go, somewhere they had to be. Who would want to listen to me? The bullhorn dropped to my side, and I stepped back against the wall.

For almost an hour I stood on that corner trying to find the courage to open my mouth. Each time I stepped forward and lifted the bullhorn, my courage would desert me and I'd step back again. I was on the verge of giving up when a voice said, 'Are you going to stand there all day? Say something!'

'Who said that?'

I looked around in amazement. There was no one standing near me, no one who looked as if they'd just spoken to me. Instead, I saw something that touched my heart. I saw the people of New York, my people, with their faces set in cold worried lines, their bodies bent against the problems life had thrown at them. I stepped forward again and lifted the bullhorn to my mouth. This time my voice rang out, 'Listen up, I've got some good news.'

The loudness of my own voice shocked me but people were stopping – I was going to have to say something.

So I continued, 'You need to have good news.'

In the crowd, one man nodded his agreement.

I opened the new pocket-sized Bible I'd bought and read, 'For God so loved the world – can you believe that God can love us? – that he sent Jesus – you've heard his name, right? – that whosoever believed in him – that's you, you're part of whosoever – would have everlasting life. Now I know that might not excite you but this will. God did not send Jesus to condemn us here in New York City, but to save us. I know how you feel today. You're lonely, depressed, you're asking where is love, why is there so much trouble in your life? Well, let me tell you, people, God sent Jesus to save us from all this!'

A large crowd had gathered by now and one man yelled out, 'Tell us some more.'

This was something I hadn't anticipated. I looked down at my Bible, back at the crowd, and down at my Bible again. I had nothing else to say – so I read the same verses over and over.

I didn't know any more. I realised then that I had to learn. I didn't know how – I couldn't even get past Genesis – but I knew I had to do it so I could help people. I left Harlem that day feeling excited, wondering what God would do next. He had given me the courage to speak, although I didn't realise at the time it was him. I thought I didn't even know how to talk to God. I thought there must be a right way to do it, but I've since found that if you just let God lead you, he'll show you the way.

After my first experience of evangelism, I went out and bought *Good News for Modern Man*, a simply translated New Testament, and I read John's Gospel again. It was to be only the beginning of my learning process.

A couple of months later, when I was out on patrol, I spotted a young Puerto Rican man giving out brochures to passers-by.

'Hey, kid, what you doing?'

'I'm handing out tracts, Officer.'

'What's a tract?'

'Here, see for yourself.'

I took the pamphlet the boy held out to me. 'You must be born again.' The words on the front cover seemed to ring a bell and I read on, finding out what it meant to be 'born again'. Excitement welled up in me as I pored over the tract.

'What's your name, kid?'

'Hector, Officer.'

'Well, Hector,' I tapped my chest and beamed at the boy, 'I'm born again.'

I had finally been able to identify what had happened to me; I could put a name to 'things', and I was delighted.

But my reaction was nothing compared to Hector's. The boy started hugging and kissing me, yelling, 'You're my brother, you're my brother.'

'Get off me,' I screamed, pushing him aside. 'What, are you crazy? If a police car passes and sees you on top of me, they won't stop and ask questions, they'll just shoot. And they might miss you and hit me!'

Hector stepped back, laughing. Two men, strangers until a moment earlier, we shook hands and slapped each other on the shoulders like brothers. Before we parted, I to continue with my beat and Hector to hand out his brochures, I said, 'Hey, give me some of those tracts. I might be able to use some.'

I didn't know it then, but those tracts were to become an integral part of my ministry. Over the years, I was to hand out thousands of them. I gave them to people on subways and in prison; I gave them to visitors to the city and vagrants; I left them on car windscreens, outside bars, anywhere I could.

I now knew the deep joy that comes from being alive in Christ, but in spite of that black depressions still descended on me. The death, the violence, the evil, the broken families and broken-hearted people that I saw in my job every day continued to bring me down, both physically and mentally. There were thousands of people in the city with problems of one kind or another, and it was as if I was taking their sorrows upon myself. I didn't know how to resolve all their problems, but the more I read the Bible the more sure I was that Jesus was the answer. But I still didn't know what I could do to help them.

Chapter 6

I was reading my Bible every day, but there was still a lot I was struggling to understand. I had no one I could ask, so going back to church seemed to be the next logical step to take. I figured that if I went to church I might find someone there who could give me answers to my questions. I'd been brought up in the Catholic religion and I didn't know anything else, so when I returned to church it was only natural that it should be the local Catholic one.

I started going along to the Sunday services. I thought it was the right thing to do, but it didn't always feel like the right thing. I'd go into a service feeling happy and I'd come out feeling there should be more to it than this. I was familiar with all the rituals and ceremony and solemnity, but I wanted more. There was a part of me that wanted to be able to shout out for joy in church and maybe even to hug people, and that definitely wasn't the sort of thing you were supposed to do.

After the service one Sunday, I stopped to talk with one of the regular church-goers.

'It's good to see you here these days, Mike,' he said. 'How you doing? Are you enjoying the services?'

'I don't know,' I said. 'It feels right to be praising God but sometimes I feel as if I'm gonna burst. I'm so happy I wanna shout out to God, or maybe lift my hands to him. Is that stupid?'

'No, Mike, of course it's not. Lots of people feel like you do, and I'm one of them.'

'What do you do about it, then?'

'Well, there's a group of us, we meet one evening a week. We all come from different Catholic churches but we get together and read the Bible and sing. We're what you'd call a charismatic group.'

'Charismatic?' I said. 'What's that mean?'

'We look at it as meaning the deep things of the Spirit.'

'The Spirit? Do you mean the Holy Ghost?'

'Yeah, the Holy Spirit of God.'

'Okay, keep talking, tell me more.'

'We pray in tongues, we practise the gifts of the Spirit, it's like nothing you'll ever have experienced in the Catholic Church before. Why don't you come along? I think you'd like it, but if you don't you don't have to come again.'

'Maybe,' I said.

I didn't know what he meant by speaking in tongues or the gifts of the Spirit – I was struggling to read and understand my Bible and I didn't have anyone to teach me – but my heart really longed to know more of the deep things of the Spirit of God. I wanted to go to their meeting, but I was still bound by all the regulations of religion that I'd been brought up with. You do things this way, our way, or you go to hell. It was as simple as that. I had to obey the rules set down by the Church. I didn't know any other way. I struggled for a long time, wanting to go to the charismatic meeting to see if there was an alternative, but I was too afraid. At last I prayed and asked God about it, and he spoke into me, saying, 'Don't you understand, you're born again? That means you don't have to obey rules made by man.'

So that evening, armed with my Bible and the courage God

54

had given me, I put on my coat ready to go to the meeting. Ann was watching me from the sofa.

'If this meeting goes on for a long time, I'll go straight to work, okay, Ann?' I said.

'Sure.' She shrugged her shoulders.

'But if I don't like it, I'll come back.'

'Okay.'

'Are you all right, Ann?'

'I'm fine.'

She picked up her sewing basket. I looked at the clock: it was time for me to go if I wanted to be on time, and I didn't want to have to walk in late so I bent over and kissed her goodbye. She didn't look up.

'Are you sure you're okay?'

'Yeah, I'm fine, just go. You don't want to be late for your meeting.'

It wasn't like Ann to sound so grumpy, but I figured she'd just had a bad day and I set off for the meeting. It was being held in a basement: when I walked down the stairs, what a sight greeted me. There were about twenty or thirty people already gathered there. Some of them had guitars and were playing quietly in the background. My friend came over and said hi, and introduced me to some of the others before we took our seats and the meeting started.

My friend was right: it was like nothing I had ever experienced in church before. This was the very early 1970s, and most churches were still very traditional in their worship: I was used to priests and nuns and candles and solemn music. But here it was guitar music, and not just that – it was lively guitar music. I liked it. I felt at home right away. I didn't care what religion said about what was proper or not; I was dying with religion. I didn't care what the priest or the cardinals or the Pope himself thought. I didn't care what anybody thought any more. I needed this.

I didn't know the songs, so I couldn't join in, but I listened to them and the words were good. There was something special here, I knew it.

Following the singing, a lady stood up. After reading from the New Testament, she spoke about what she had read. She was an ordinary woman, dressed in normal clothes, but the words she spoke had an extraordinary impact on me. She talked about heaven. Now I'd spent all my life learning about hell, but I'd never given heaven a thought. I'd always been hell-bound, and even though I was now born again I still believed that I was going to hell. I loved Jesus, but I didn't expect him to take me to heaven; I was content to be happy on earth, which was way more than I'd been a few weeks earlier.

Even though Jesus had saved me from the brink of the pit of hell I'd seen in the vision I'd had during my recovery from the head injury, I hadn't really understood what he meant when he said, 'You don't belong in there, you belong with me.' I still believed there was nothing I could do to avoid hell. I certainly didn't realise that I was already saved from that destination and that I was going to heaven.

As the woman spoke, God gave me another vision. I was aware of what she was saying, but it was as if I was in a different dimension. I was in a beautiful place where the streets were made of gold. It wasn't any place I recognised: certainly not New York, where many of the streets were dirty and covered in garbage. In my vision I saw trees of many different colours: pinks and yellows and reds and colours I didn't recognise, colours I'd never seen before, wonderful colours. Then I was in the picture, walking down the street. Suddenly two hands grabbed mine. I didn't see a face but I saw a white robe with golden lace around it, and a voice said, 'I know your troubles, I know what you went through. It was I, Jesus, who delivered you. You will do great exploits for me.'

Then I was back in the room and the woman was finishing speaking.

At the end of the meeting my friend said, 'Well, what did you think, Mike? Will you come back again?'

'Try stopping me,' I grinned.

I couldn't wait for these weekly meetings. I soon learned the songs and I'd sing them round the house and in the car. I was so happy. The only thing spoiling my joy was the fact that Ann didn't want to come with me, didn't even want to know. The happier I was, it seemed the more miserable Ann got.

While I was out on the street seeing all kinds of things which could bring my morale down, Ann was under different sorts of pressures. It's tough being a cop's wife. Your husband works long shifts, sometimes at night and often over holiday periods when everyone else seems to be home enjoying themselves. And added to that, there's always the possibility that it will be your husband who gets shot today. You hear a report on the radio of a policeman injured in the line of duty and you wait, your heart in your mouth, to hear from your man, to hear him say, 'It's okay, honey, I'm all right. It's not me who got beat up today.' It can be lonely being a cop's wife. I hated seeing Ann looking so miserable.

One evening I was going up the stairs to our apartment when Ann came down on her way out. She was huffy.

'Look at you with that Bible! No one wants to talk to me any more. That's the trouble with you, every time you do something you gotta go all the way with it. Well, you'd better snap out of it, cos I've had enough!'

'Ann, there's nothing I can do. I don't know what's happening myself. I just see God doing things for me and it's overwhelming me. I can't help myself.'

'Well, you'd better try.'

She pushed past me and carried on down the stairs. It wasn't like her to act like that, and I felt bad. I asked God about it. I said, 'Lord, what's happening to Ann and me? We're splitting apart, going our separate ways. Is that what you want? We've been so happy together until now.' I didn't think that God

57

would want us to grow apart, but I couldn't see what other choice there was.

Ann wasn't home before I went to work, and that wasn't like her either. I went off feeling uncertain.

I did my shift, and when I got home I found Ann sitting up in bed with a Bible. We looked at each other.

'Mike, I want to ask you a question.'

I didn't say anything. I was still upset that she'd pushed me on the stairs and I didn't really want to answer her question; I wanted an apology. But in my head I heard the Holy Spirit ask, 'Do you want an apology or do you want your wife saved?'

I admit I had to think about that for a moment, but finally I said, 'I want my wife saved.'

'Then quiet up and listen to her.'

While this was going on in my head, Ann was waiting. I said, 'Go on, Ann, what do you want to ask me?'

'Do you really believe that what we learnt about Jesus being God is true and that he loves us?'

'That's been my experience for the last five months.'

'Mike, I've been so miserable these last few weeks. I've hated seeing you get so happy while I've been so miserable. I can see what's happened to you, how you've changed. I'd love this to happen to me.'

'Do you want me to explain to you what I learned?'

'Sure.'

'Okay, well, there's something called the sinner's prayer.'

'What's that?'

'Well, we hold hands and we admit that we're sinners and we ask Jesus to take over our life and our will.'

'Jesus takes over our life? What's that mean?'

'I don't rightly know but I like it. I don't know how he does it, I'm still learning myself, but I do know this: he will change us and transform our lives.'

'I'd like that.'

'Come on, then.'

I sat on the bed next to Ann and we held hands and prayed. I said the words and Ann said them after me. It was a great feeling. I knew then that God wanted us to be together with him for ever. The two truly became one in him.

And that night a strange thing happened. Ann instantly knew there were things in our apartment that weren't godly. We had some pictures that were fashionable at the time but which contained occult symbols. Ann took them down and threw them out. She went all round the apartment, clearing out anything that she felt was wrong. I've read since, in the Bible, in the book of Acts, of the way the early Christians did the same thing. We had our own little book of Acts that night.

Ever since then, Ann has been, and continues to be, the heart of my ministry. But alongside that, she has her own ministry, which has grown over the years. She's worked with kids in the ghettos, running vacation Bible clubs, she's ministered to thousands of cops' wives, and she plays an important role in the Cops for Christ organisation, as secretary.

About seven months after I was saved, I heard someone speak about water baptism, the kind where someone is totally immersed in the water, just like in the days of the early Church. Before Jesus began his ministry, he was baptised by John the Baptist.

The pastor explained that salvation didn't depend on being baptised but that it was symbolic. He said, 'When you go under the water, your old life passes away, and you come up out of the water to your new life.' I listened to him and I heard God tell me to do it, but I wasn't sure what people would think about me. I had to make a decision. My parents had had me christened as a baby, when I'd been sprinkled with a few drops of water: did I really need to do this now? But I wanted to listen to God and obey what he put on my heart, I wanted to make that commitment. So I said, 'Well, if it was good enough for the early Church, then it's good enough for me.'

Ann and I decided to be baptised together, and one bitterly

cold evening in October a group of about a hundred of our family and friends gathered beside a swimming pool to watch our baptism. As we all stood around beforehand, praising God, our faces were masked by the vapour coming out of our mouths, it was so cold. Then it was time for Ann and me to go in the pool. We held hands and went down under the water together. It was a beautiful experience and we had such a sense of peace through it, a sense of obedience to God. It was such a great feeling it even overcame the freezing cold creeping up my spine!

There are plenty of books and commentaries that explain words and stories in the Bible, but sometimes just reading the Bible and letting God speak can bring the greatest revelation. With water baptism, God settled it in my spirit and I did it, and that was the start of my obedience to God. It was the beginning of me being set free from worrying about what man thought; I simply wanted to do what God told me to do.

I continued to attend the charismatic Catholic group at St Lawrence in Sayville, the only difference being that now Ann came with me. And what a difference it was! My joy was complete now we were sharing everything.

It was exciting because I was learning so much all the time. One evening, another lady got up in the meeting to speak. She spoke about what the Bible says about baptism in the Holy Spirit. I'd been baptised in water but this was something different. She read from the book of Acts where the apostle Paul is filled with the Spirit of God. I'd read it in the Bible myself but I didn't know what it meant.

The woman said, 'Why don't you, for just once in your life, not worry about what people say or what they think? Forget what your religion says, just step out in faith and listen to what God says to you.'

She wasn't addressing me personally – there were about fifty people in the room – but God used her words to speak to me.

I was going to do what she said, not because she'd said it but because God said, 'Do this.' I knew Jesus was my friend and I was beginning to feel the presence of God in my life more and more, but I knew I needed something extra. I was losing confidence in my ability to do my job, and my self-esteem was dropping down again. I decided I was going to do what God said.

I went out to the front and sat on a chair. The speaker and some others gathered around me.

'We're going to pray over you,' one of them said, 'and ask Jesus to baptise you with his Holy Spirit.'

I took comfort in the fact that it was Jesus, my best buddy, who was going to do the job, and I said, 'Let's go for it, then.'

As they prayed, I felt very close to Jesus. I knew by faith that God was with me. The Bible tells us that the disciples, after they'd been filled with the Holy Spirit, spoke in strange languages and people were amazed. After my baptism, I spoke in a heavenly language for the first time. It was only one word, but I felt so good doing it. I didn't know it then, but I was going to use this language many times when I was in difficult and dangerous situations and I needed to cry out to God.

That night I headed off for work with an added joy. I had a new confidence. Where just hours before I'd been afraid of losing it, now I knew I couldn't. My self-esteem had gone back up because Jesus was with me. I'm not a big guy – at the time I weighed about 145 pounds – and now I felt like David fighting Goliath, knowing that no matter what situation I had to face, Jesus was with me. This wasn't an ego trip to make me feel good, but a confidence trip to enable me to go on with my job. Without it I most probably would have quit the police force.

Chapter 7

'Mike, I've been thinking.'

I looked at Ann across the dinner table. We'd just finished eating.

'Oh yeah, what you been thinking about, honey?'

'What about having a Bible study here and inviting our friends and people we know from the neighbourhood?'

'Yeah, that would be good. But who would we get to lead it?'

'You, Mike.'

'Me!' I spluttered over my coffee. 'You gotta be joking!'

I looked at Ann to see if she was serious. She was. Her face was earnest and her eyes were shining.

'You could do it, Mike, I know you could.'

'Ann, honey, you know I don't have any education. I can't put two big words together. Who's gonna want to listen to someone like me?'

'People like us, Mike. The people I've invited don't know anything about God. They certainly don't know any more than we do.'

'Whadya mean – "the people I've invited"? You mean you've already invited people?'

'Look, Mike, there are so many hurting people out there. I love them, you love them, and you've got a heart for them. You're learning the Bible – who can teach fellow New Yorkers better than us? And who else would want to come in here and teach these people?'

I thought about what she said for a minute. It made sense. 'Okay, we'll do it.'

'Thanks, Mike, I knew you'd do it. It's this Friday.'

'Whaaaat?'

I got up from the table. I knew there was no use arguing with Ann when she was set on something.

'I'd better start preparing right now,' I said.

I had learned some more of the Bible since my first attempt at street evangelism, when I'd only known two verses. I'd been trying to tune in my radio one day, looking for a music station, when a voice had come over the airwaves saying, 'You must be born again.' My ears twitched. I recognised that phrase. I played with the dial a bit more until I could hear the man speaking clearly. He was talking about the word of God. When he'd finished, he said, 'If you want to learn more about the word of God, why not do our correspondence course? It's written in easy-to-understand language for the man in the street. If you would like more information, send your name and address to us and we'll send you a trial lesson.' Then he gave their name and their address before some more music was played. I'd lost interest in finding a music station: I was much more interested in finding out about the Bible study. I thought about it – I really wanted to learn more about the Bible but my confidence in my ability to study was still low. I asked Ann if she thought I would be able to do a correspondence course.

'Of course, you could, Mike. If you want to learn, then you'll be able to do it. Anyway, it won't hurt to send for the trial lesson.'

She was right, as usual, and soon I was working my way through the lessons, so when she suggested the Bible study I did at least have some knowledge that I thought I could share with others.

Fifty-two people gathered in our home for our first Bible study. I couldn't believe that so many were interested – or that we could get so many in our place! Ann had put out some potato chips and pretzels, as we wanted people to socialise and relax for a while and I wanted to put off the time when I had to speak. I was real nervous.

After about an hour, people were starting to look restless. They hadn't come here for a party, they'd come for a different reason. I cleared my throat and called for their attention. I had prepared something from the Bible to teach them, but then God said to me, 'Share your life with them, Mike, tell them what you've been through.'

'Naah, why would they wanna hear that?'

'Because they've been through the same things, they'll understand what you're talking about.'

That made sense so I did what God said. I talked about growing up in the Bronx, my experience of the violence I saw as a child, how I'd met the policeman who'd got me off the streets, then how I'd met my wife and, finally, how I'd met Jesus.

'We all go through struggles,' I said, 'and we don't know how to share them. We keep our experiences hidden inside ourselves, we don't want to tell others about them in case we seem weak. I'm the same as the rest of you, I've had my troubles, but I've found that the answer to my problems is Jesus.'

As I was talking, I noticed some people were crying. I thought I must have said something to offend them or hurt them, and I was really glad when the meeting finished. After the last person had left, I shut the door and said to Ann, 'Oh boy, I'm glad that's over.'

'Why? You did great.'

'But Ann, didn't you see? There were people crying. What did I say to offend them?'

'They weren't offended, Mike, they were touched by what you said.'

'Touched? But there were guys crying. New York guys don't cry.'

'They cried because they identified with your experiences.'

'You sure? They weren't offended?'

'Honest, Mike, it was good. Besides, you can ask them yourself when they come back next week.'

'Whaaat? They're coming back next week?'

That Bible study turned out to be the start of a church, although we didn't know it then and we wouldn't have called it a church because we still thought that a church was a building. We didn't realise then that it's the people that make a church of God. There was a lot we didn't know back then, but it wasn't important; all that was important was that we knew Jesus.

Within eighteen months from that small beginning, there were three hundred people coming along to the meetings. We had to rent a nearby building. As well as our neighbours and friends, the meetings attracted alcoholics, drug addicts and prostitutes, and God saw our hearts and worked many miracles. We saw alcoholics and addicts cured of their addictions, many sick and seriously ill healed, and prostitutes giving up their life on the street. They were all changed by the power of God. We saw many more people in tears, and my own tears would be enough to fill New York's East River.

While it was great to see so many people coming to know God, the strain was beginning to tell on me. One group of people depended on me in my role as church leader, and another group depended on me to be a police officer. Being a cop requires top physical condition. We're involved in hand-to-hand, as well as armed, combat and we have to be alert at all times. If we're less than 100 per cent, we put our partner's life at risk as well as our own. I was physically very tired. Trying to keep going in my two roles meant I was only getting about three or four hours' sleep a day, and it was having an effect on my body. I realised that I had to make a decision. I could either step back from a position of leadership in the church or I could quit the police. I asked the Lord what I should do. I said, 'Should I leave the police department and become a full-time Christian leader?'

I knew I had to make a decision, but I knew that God would give me clear guidance. Even when we don't know what to do, we can be sure that he does, and I left my problem with him and waited for his answer.

Meanwhile, back in the police force life went on as normal in New York City. That meant anything from dealing with drunks to catching robbers or apprehending murderers. I had a young cop working with me then. His name was Joey. We had become friendly, and I was teaching him all I knew about being a cop in New York. One night he arrested an armed man and took him back to the precinct for processing. As we finished our tour of duty that night he said, 'Okay, Mike, see ya. I've gotta be in court tomorrow, remember.'

'Yeah, fine, Joey, take care.'

I went home and grabbed a couple of hours' sleep. When I got up, Ann was getting ready to do some grocery shopping. She picked up her purse, kissed me goodbye and left. About twenty minutes later I heard the front door of our apartment opening. I looked up and was surprised to see Ann standing there.

'Hi, honey, that was quick,' I said. I looked at her shopping bag, which was hanging empty at her side. 'Didn't they have what you needed?'

'Come here, Mike.' She held out her arms to me.

I got up and walked over to her.

'What's the matter, Ann?'

She put her arms around me.

'Mike, Joey's been killed.'

'Joey? Naah, that can't be right.'

'It is, Mike, I just heard it on the radio.'

'Naah, they've got it wrong. Joey made an arrest last night and he was going to be in court today.'

'Mike, it just came on the news. Why don't you phone the district?'

I did as Ann suggested and called the district. The desk sergeant answered the phone.

'It's Mike DiSanza, Sarge . . .'

He interrupted me.

'Yeah, Mike, we figured you'd call. Come on down.'

It was true, then. I still couldn't believe it. He was only a young kid, not long on the force. I made my way down to the district and went in to see the captain, who told me what appeared to have happened. Joey had come home from court and was off duty. He'd been at a subway station when someone had produced a gun. A woman had yelled and the gunman had run away, with Joey following him up the subway steps. At the top, the gunman had spotted two policemen and had yelled to them, 'There's a madman following me with a gun.' Joey had appeared at the top of the stairs, his gun in his hand, and the policemen had fired at him and killed him. They hadn't noticed the police badge he was holding out to identify himself. It was a great tragedy, both for Joey and his family and for the cops who'd had to react quickly in the face of possible danger, and had been forced to shoot.

My young friend was dead, and I had to come to terms with it. I went home feeling disturbed and very upset.

That night I couldn't sleep. I went out on to the fire escape from our apartment and looked out at the streets. It was a clear starry night, and looking up at the sky that was so beautiful it was hard to believe that there could be anything wrong in the world. The nights are never completely quiet in New York; there's always some noise in the distance, the hum of traffic or raised voices. That night, though, I didn't hear anything as I stood on the balcony; my head was too full of thoughts of Joey.

As I stood there, deep in thought, out of the darkness thousands of hideous creatures came flying at me, right up close. I stepped back against the wall, horrified. In the midst of these monsters was one larger, even more evil-looking creature. He came right up in front of my face. I could smell his vile breath as he screamed at me, 'We declare war on you!'

The air all around me was full of oppression, and I could feel it closing in, weakening my will, filling me with fear. I could hear the buzz of murmuring from these creatures, and the pressure on my chest was becoming unbearable when suddenly a strong loud voice came from deep within me, 'No, we declare war on you!'

As soon as those words were spoken, they all dispersed: all the demons went fleeing back to the darkness out of which they'd come, and the oppression on me was gone. The sudden relief from the pressure on my body made me fall forwards against the fire escape railings, and I stood there, slumped over, grabbing on to the metal bars. My heart was pounding and I was sweating profusely. What had happened to me?

God gave me the answer to that question. The Holy Spirit spoke to my spirit and said, 'Those creatures tonight were evil spirits, the spirits of murder, rape, robbery, oppression, addiction. These are the demons you will have to face if you stay in the police force. But I tell you that if you defend my name in this city, then I will defend you. I will give you the grace to get by and you will be a blessing to others. If you stay a year in the police force, I'll give you a city; five years, a nation; and if you spend your career there, I'll give you many nations.'

I didn't understand at that time what God meant when he spoke of cities and nations, but I knew then and there that he wanted me to stay in the police rather than go into full-time Christian ministry. The Bible tells us to 'make sure your election and calling is sure'. It was sure now, and I knew that God would keep his promise to protect me. He hadn't brought about the tragedy of Joey's murder – it's the devil that brings tragedy – but God could make good out of it.

The next morning I went to see the captain. He was a born-again Christian and I had confided in him previously that I was thinking about leaving the police. Now I told him what had happened the night before and what God had put on my heart.

'Mike, I'm glad you're staying,' he said. 'Boy, do we need a witness in this city.'

'Thanks, Captain, but there's something else.'

'What's that?'

'I believe God wants me to work steady nights here in Harlem.'

I knew as well as anyone that it was a hard area to work in, but I felt that I was already making some headway. One really cold night I was patrolling 125th Street and saw a crowd of guys gathered round an old fifty-gallon steel drum. They'd lit a fire in it and were feeding it with everything they could find to keep warm. I felt the Holy Spirit say to me, 'Go over and talk to those guys.' I walked over to join them.

'Hi guys, sure is cold tonight. Mind if I join you?'

I put my hands out over the fire and rubbed them together.

'Man, we don't want no pigs here.'

'Don't worry, guys, I'm just trying to get a little heat.'

'Aw, he's all right, let him get warm.'

'Why's he want to come here?'

'Maybe he just wants our company, let him alone.'

They started talking then about other things, and I knew it was going to be all right. I introduced myself to them, and we started to get to know each other. The next night I went back again to the fire, we talked some more, and I started telling them a bit about my life. They understood where I was coming from, the sort of place I'd grown up in.

'Hey, man, you're cool, you're all right for a cop.'

Little by little, night by night, I told them more about my life, and then about meeting Jesus and the new hope he had given me. These people hadn't had any good news for a long time: they needed someone there to bring them some, and I believed that God was telling me to be that person, to be available in the night-times when there was no one else around. But the captain had other ideas.

'No, Mike, you can't do that,' he said. 'Straight nights are too much for anyone to take. It's not good policy. No matter what you feel now, you don't realise what you're saying – it could overwhelm you.'

'But, Captain, in the night-times, in the dark, that's when there's the most trouble, when the most hurting people are, and there's no witness for God, no one to tell them it could be different. The Pope's in bed, Billy Graham's in bed, there's no one out there. The Lord said, "Whom shall I send?" and like Isaiah (Isaiah 6:8) I said, "Send me." I believe the Lord wants me to be there and he has promised to help me survive.'

The captain still wasn't convinced, but at last we compromised.

'Okay, Mike, if you're so sure, we'll give it six months, but if at any time you feel you can't handle it any more, just tell me and we'll reassign you.'

I agreed to that six-month trial period – I didn't know, but maybe the Lord just wanted me to work nights for a short time. I ended up on night tours for most of my career.

Chapter 8

Some kind of trouble would happen most nights when I was on duty. Sure, there were boring times in every tour of duty, but most nights there'd be some occurrence or other. Although these were usually bad, sometimes, just sometimes, good things happened too.

One night after arresting a suspect, I had to take him back to the precinct for processing. There I led him into a small back room and took his finger-prints. It's a messy job, finger-printing. No matter how careful I was, I always managed to get ink on my fingers. After we'd finished, I took my prisoner back to his cell, then went to the rest-room to clean my hands. The rest-room was down a dark dingy corridor, and on one of the walls there was a bulletin board that the guys used to advertise items they had for sale or events that were happening. I usually glanced at the board as I passed, in case there was something interesting going on, and on this particular night one of the notices caught my eye. The board was crowded, covered with lots of these little white index cards, but it was just one of them that stood out for me. I stopped and read it.

It was the first line that grabbed my attention. It said, 'Anyone interested in praying . . .'

I couldn't believe my eyes. 'Praying,' I thought, 'praying? A notice about praying on a police bulletin board? Wow, what's this about?'

I hurried to read on. It was an invitation to a prayer meeting in a church hall in Brooklyn a few days later. The bulletin board wasn't in a public place – it was only accessible to cops – so I knew the card had to have been put there by a police officer. I was overwhelmed. Cops meeting to pray. Wow! There and then my heart started thumping as I felt the power of the Holy Spirit charging through my body. I didn't know who was involved or what they were going to be praying about, but I knew this had to be good. I couldn't wait to find out more.

The day of the prayer meeting arrived. I was working the night before and I'd asked Ann to make sure I got up in plenty of time. She came into the bedroom and woke me. I was so excited, I said, 'Ann, today's the day. I can't wait.' Ann smiled at me but she had a worried look on her face.

'What's the matter, Ann?'

She shook her head. 'There's a problem, Mike.'

'Whad'ya mean, a problem?'

'There's been a big snowstorm while you've been asleep. All the roads are going to be real hard to get through. There've been warnings on the radio advising motorists not to travel.'

'Oh no,' I said, 'not today, of all days. What if they cancel the meeting? Or what if they set a new date, how will I get to know about it? I don't know who's arranging it or anything. I gotta go to this meeting, Ann.'

'But honey, you said yourself, they'll probably cancel it.'

'I don't care, I've gotta try. I might not have another chance.'

The meeting was scheduled to start at 7.30 that evening. It was in Brooklyn and I was in the Bronx. It wasn't that far, but I knew it was going to take me some time with the roads as bad as they were. The car we owned then was a yellow Volkswagen Beetle, and at four o'clock in the afternoon I got into it and started out for the meeting. We were into blizzard conditions now, but the little bug was a reliable car and it went pretty good. To get to Brooklyn I had to go from one end of the city to the other, right through Manhattan and across the Brooklyn Bridge. The weather was so bad that cars were stuck in the snow and even buses were stalled. Sometimes the car would skid sideways or it'd go up on the sidewalk, but I was young and I was having fun. I put the siren going on the car's roof, *whee*, *whee*, and I sat back and enjoyed myself. The only thing that was bothering me was how long the journey was taking. I kept looking at my watch. Time was going by, and I didn't want to be late or to miss the meeting altogether. At last, nearly three and a half hours after I'd set off, I finally got there. At 7.20 exactly, I pulled up outside the Catholic church hall where the meeting was supposed to be held, only to find it in total darkness.

'Oh, no,' I cried, 'don't tell me they cancelled it!'

Then another idea struck me. What if I had the wrong address?

But I'd come a long way and I wasn't going to give up that easily. I figured as I was there I might as well take a look around. It was a dangerous area, and I got out of the car cautiously. It didn't look too good – the windows of the church were boarded up and there was no sign of life anywhere. I walked along the front of the church and peered down the alley at the side. I could see a faint light in the darkness. I went to check it out. It was coming from inside the church, through a side door that was very slightly ajar. I pushed it open some more and it creaked on its ancient hinges. I stuck my head in, and when my eyes had got accustomed to the light I could see four men, their eyes closed, standing in a circle holding hands. The room appeared to be unheated, and it was so cold I could see the vapour rising out of their mouths. I went in, pushed the door closed behind me – we didn't need to let any more cold in – and walked over to join the circle. As I got closer I realised they were praying – and not only that, they were praying for cops in New York City. As they became aware of my presence, two of the guys let go of their hands and moved over to make room for me. I joined the group and we continued to pray. Each of us prayed for our own specific area, then we prayed for the city, and then we prayed for the country.

As I stood there with these other guys, all the tension of my trip faded away. I felt both excited and at peace. This was the place to be. I didn't know where it was going or whether we would ever meet again, but it didn't matter – at that moment it was just the right place to be.

After we'd finished, we introduced ourselves. A couple of the guys already knew each other, but the rest of us were strangers until then. We talked a little about ourselves and the areas we worked and the need there was for prayer. Then one of the guys said, 'Hey, we should meet again next month.'

As he said that it was like a surge of electricity ran right through me, I was so excited. We were going to do this again. Cops were going to meet and pray again.

We met again the next month, and the month after that. Each time a few more cops would have heard about it and they'd come along. Within six months, there were a hundred police officers coming to the prayer meetings. We eventually had to rent a building in Queens for this bunch of New York City cops to meet and pray.

Some time after that, a policeman in New Jersey was killed in a tragic incident. The state of New Jersey is on the other side of the Hudson River from New York City, and a Christian cop there had heard through the grapevine about us. He contacted us and asked us to pray about this situation and for all those involved. We did as he asked, and as we did so we saw the need for cops who will pray not just in NYC, but everywhere. We encouraged our New Jersey friend and helped him to set up a similar movement in his area.

We didn't know then what plans God had for us, but we knew this was getting bigger than just a few guys meeting up now and then, and we realised that it needed to be done properly. One of the first things we decided was that we needed a name. Those who led the NYC group met and prayed about choosing the right name, then we sat and discussed it.

'Christian Policemen Association?'

'Naah.'

'Policemen for Jesus?'

'Maybe.'

'Cops for Jesus?'

'No, but whadabout – Cops for Christ!'

'That's it!'

We all agreed, and in 1974 Cops for Christ started officially. Within a very short period of time there were chapters of Cops for Christ springing up all over New England – in Connecticut, Massachusetts, Maine – and then in other parts of the States as well. It seemed like everywhere there were groups of cops praying. From the east coast of America to the west we were taking phone calls from police departments wanting to get involved, and a number of us spent time travelling round talking to policemen, telling them how to set up a chapter in their own area.

As well as meeting to pray, we began a more evangelistic work, speaking at meetings, in schools and in prisons. We also produced our own radio programme. Every Saturday evening we broadcast a half-hour slot on a Christian radio station. We had purchased radio time, and now we could use it to share our message over the airwaves. We'd preach a little, or sometimes we'd interview people or ask them to give their own testimony. As well as hearing from police officers, we had ex-addicts, ex-Mafioso, ex-prostitutes, all coming on and telling the listeners how God had saved them. At the end we'd give out a telephone number for anyone listening who might be interested to find out more.

One night after the broadcast we had a call from a German policeman. He had heard the broadcast and he wanted to start something similar to Cops for Christ in Germany. As a result of that phone call, a couple of our guys were sponsored by other Christian ministries to go over to Germany to set up our first international chapter.

Within a relatively short period of time, Cops for Christ progressed from being a small local group to a world-wide organisation, who have since won thousands upon thousands for Christ. I've learned not to despise small beginnings, because I know God doesn't.

A short time later, a 'New England for Jesus' crusade was held in Massachusetts, and Cops for Christ was invited to send a team to be part of the rally in Boston. Fifty-two of us made the five-hour journey up there from New York on a chartered bus. Some of the guys had brought their guitars, one had even brought a battery-operated keyboard, and during the journey we sang and enjoyed being in each other's company. I was having a great time just relaxing with other guys who knew Jesus. After a while the bus fell silent, everyone deep in their own thoughts, and then one of the cops, a guy called Carlos, got up. He made his way to the front of the bus, picked up the driver's microphone, then turned and started to talk.

'Did I ever tell you guys my testimony, how I got saved, how God moved in my life?'

Most of us had heard Carlos's story before, but there were a few who hadn't. I could see his eyes take on a distant look as he remembered the past and told us his story.

'You all know I'm Puerto Rican, but did you know I used to be a gang leader? I was notorious in the Bronx as a tough guy. No one messed with me.'

I knew what he said was true. All the guys who worked with Carlos knew that he was a tough boy.

'Well, one day, me and my boys were walking down the street. When people saw us coming, they usually got out of the way, but this time, a girl was walking towards us and she didn't move over to let me pass. I had to get out of her way. When the guys saw me moving out of her way, they said, "Hey, Carlos man, why you let that girl make you move you like that?"

'I said, "Don't worry, it won't happen again. No girl's gonna do that to Carlos."

'Next day we saw her coming down the street again. I thought, this is it, she's gonna get out of my way this time. But she didn't. I had to move again. "Hey, Carlos," the guys said to me, "don't she know who you are, man?"

'I said, "Hey, girl, don't you know who I am?" and she said, "Sure, everyone knows who you are, you're Carlos."

' "Then why didn't you move out of my way, girl?"

'Then she said, "Why should I move out of your way? Don't you know who I am?"

'The guys looked at me and I looked at her. I said, "What you talking about, girl? I don't know you."

' "Well, I'm a child of God and I'm not scared of you guys," she said, and then this little bit of a girl starts telling me and my boys about God and how much Jesus loves us. D'ya know what happened then? I got saved, and what's more, some time later, I married that very same girl.'

A big cheer went up from the guys on the bus. It was a great story. We all knew Carlos was a fine cop. He was able to help many people because he could identify with many of the situations they were in – he'd been there himself.

The bus rolled on, the guys sitting back thinking about what Carlos had said, and then Danny got up. He was a big guy, about 290 pounds, and he was sweating slightly. He walked to the front, took the microphone, took his hat off and began to talk.

'I used to be an alcoholic. Some of you will remember how I used to be in those days. An alcoholic cop. I'm not proud of that. I don't know how I managed to keep my job. People covered up for me, I guess, but I was losing my family because of my drinking. My wife was threatening to leave me and take our five kids with her. I was in the pits. I thought drink was the only way out, but the more I drank the more my life was falling apart. My drinking was getting completely out of control. Until I met him.'

Danny pointed at me.

'Mikey talked to me about Jesus and I got saved. The Lord released me from drinking, my wife stayed with me, and now we got eight kids!'

Another cheer went up. Even though I'd heard these things before, it was great to be reminded of God's goodness. We sang a few more songs and then another couple of guys stood up and shared their stories about what God had done for them. Then Bill got up. He was the President of Cops for Christ at the time.

'I've been sitting here, quietly thinking,' he said, 'about what God has done in these lives, in all our lives. I remember when Cops for Christ started, a couple of years ago, with just a few of us meeting in a hall, and now look at what's been accomplished – souls saved, families reunited. I have to tell you it's an honour to be with you guys.'

Bill was making his way back to his seat when he stumbled as the bus pulled over to the side suddenly. We looked at each other, puzzled. It wasn't a gas station; we appeared to have stopped on the side of the highway in the middle of nowhere. The bus driver switched off the engine and stood up. He took off his hat and held it across his chest. The night was drawing in and it was very dark in the bus. I could only see his silhouette and his eyes. He looked around the bus, at all of us who were waiting, wondering what was going on, and he said, 'I just want you policemen to know that I have never heard anything like this in my life. I want this Jesus, the one you're talking about.'

The words were hardly out of his mouth before fifty-two guys had leapt up and tried to run down the narrow aisle of the bus towards him. We prayed for him and he got saved. Each testimony, each song had played its part in helping the bus driver come to know Jesus, as the power of God worked through people who loved him.

We were a happy crowd when we set off from New York City, but it was an even happier bunch of guys who finally arrived at Boston for the rally.

The crusade was taking place on the Boston Commons, the scene of much fighting during the American War of Independence. This day there must have been about 175,000 people sitting all over the park. Our group was sitting on the stage at the front. Looking around, all I could see was faces, smiling happy faces everywhere. On the stage with us were some musicians with guitars, drums and keyboards, and it was their job to lead the worship. They started to play and we all joined in with the singing, but I was so full of joy I just wanted to express it some other way. I had a tambourine in my hand, and after a while I stood up – we were all still sitting down at that point – and I began to shake my tambourine and to dance with the music. Within seconds, all the other cops were up on their feet, dancing and moving round and praising God. After that, there was no stopping us. The whole crowd of people throughout the park began dancing to the music and worshipping God. The Holy Spirit brought 'joy unspeakable' to the people that day. The worship and praying went on for a long time, much longer than had been planned, but at last it quietened down. Then Bill got up to speak. He explained who he was and what Cops for Christ was about, and then he called up the bus driver, saying, 'I'd like you to meet someone who's got something he wants to tell you.'

The bus driver made his way to the front of the stage, holding his hat in his hands again, and he shouted into the microphone, 'I've just met Jesus.'

The whole park erupted, with people cheering and shouting for joy, and the bus driver, beaming all over his face, stood and waved to everyone. When at last some quiet was restored, he went on to tell the crowds, very simply, what had happened to him while driving his bus up to Boston. The guy had been a Christian for a couple of hours and he'd already given his testimony to thousands of people – you could call it a baptism of fire!

Later on, after the rally ended, Bill called us together. He said, 'Guys, I know you're tired and you want to get home soon, but we've been invited to a dinner.'

'Oh, not now, Bill! Where's it gonna be?'

'Well, this is kinda a special dinner. It's a little distance from here; there will be one thousand Catholics there, and they'd like us to speak.'

'Whoa, okay, that is special.'

I don't know what those Catholics who attended the dinner were expecting, but God stepped in. Bill spoke first, then he introduced the bus driver, then Carlos gave his testimony and finally I addressed the guests. It was a time when the people there needed hope, and the Holy Spirit moved powerfully and did some great work among them. These were conservative people, but before I finished my message people moved the tables away and got up to dance and sing. I have never experienced such a joyful moment in my life – Catholic nuns in their habits dancing with the joy of God. Alleluia!

Just off the north shore of the borough of Queens is Rikers Island, home to the city's largest prison. One day in December in the late 1970s, one of the correction cops, whose job it is to watch over the prisoners, contacted Cops for Christ and asked if we'd be interested in doing a rally for the prisoners on Christmas Eve. My first thought was: how many guys are going to want to give up time they could be spending with their families at this special season to go and minister to inmates? It was bad timing. The journey there and back and the meeting would between them take at least six hours, probably more with all the traffic on the roads. Plus Christmas Eve was a difficult day to give up, especially for cops who rarely get a Christmas off. But, to my amazement, about thirty guys volunteered, some coming from as far as Connecticut and Pennsylvania.

So that Christmas Eve a group of uniformed cops went to prison. With some uneasiness we walked into the meeting hall, where the inmates were already gathered, only to be greeted by jeers and shouts of, 'Hey, pigs,' and 'Oink, oink'. It wasn't the warmest of welcomes!

Not surprisingly, most prisoners aren't very fond of policemen, but every seat in the hall was taken for our meeting. The chaplain said afterwards that he'd never seen so many attend a church service. Some people probably came because they were interested to hear what cops had to say, but more probably came along because of the season. At Christmas people do think a little more about God; and it is a family time and these guys were separated from their loved ones. Whatever their reason for being there, they were making plenty of noise as we arrived and they continued to heckle us as we made our way to the front.

The prison chaplain introduced us and tried to enforce some kind of order and quiet, but the murmurs and noise continued. Then one of the black cops picked up his trombone and began to play 'Silent Night'. Within seconds the heckling stopped, and by the time he finished playing there was complete silence. Many people had their heads bent down, some in tears, when Bill got up to speak.

He said, 'These guys have given up their Christmas Eve to be here with you, so be patient and listen to them. If you don't like what they have to say, that's fine, we'll be leaving soon, but just give us a chance, okay?'

A couple of the cops gave short testimonies and another one sang a solo. I could see from their faces that some of the guys in the audience were amazed to hear policemen admitting that they had had problems and gone through hard times. When it was my turn I told them a little of my story and shared some words from the Bible. After that Bill got up again and spoke. He said, 'How many of you guys would really like to ask Jesus, today, to forgive all the sins you've ever committed? Would you stand up now please, if you'd like to invite him into your hearts?'

There must have been about nine hundred in the audience that day. About half of them stood up, and I believe many more who didn't want to stand probably said the words of the prayer as well.

Good as that story is, it doesn't end there. About seventeen years later, as a representative of Cops for Christ, I was one of the guest speakers at a Chuck Colson Ministries rally in Florida. Chuck Colson was President Nixon's right-hand man, and he was one of those who went to prison as a result of the Watergate affair. While he was inside, he got saved, and when he came out he started a prison ministry that today is international.

This day there were about three hundred people at the rally I was addressing in one of Florida's parks. I was about five minutes into my testimony when a guy came up on to the platform. He walked up to me, put his arms around me and hugged me. Plenty of unexpected things have happened to me during my Christian life so I wasn't fazed by this, I just waited to find out what it was about. At last he let go of me and said, 'Can I share something? Do you mind?'

'Not at all, go ahead.' I gave him the microphone and he began to speak to the crowd.

'Seventeen years ago I was a prisoner on Rikers Island. One Christmas Eve this fellow came in with a group of other cops. He gave his testimony and I was saved that day.'

A big cheer went up from the crowd, and the man went on to say how, led by the Holy Spirit, he'd begun to read the Bible, and that when he got out of prison he began to attend church regularly.

'And now I'm a part of Chuck Colson Ministries.'

When Cops for Christ went into Rikers Island for that Christmas Eve meeting, we had no way of following up on any of the inmates. What happened to them was out of our hands, but they were in safer hands than ours. God always follows up.

Chapter 9

Sometimes I worked my tour of duty alone, sometimes with a partner – it all depended on the manpower available in the district. Jimmy and I were regular partners for many years, and this developed into a close friendship. Because our lives were regularly put at risk, it was natural for us to grow close to one another, and a very special camaraderie developed. Jimmy was as close a friend as anyone could ever have. We were part of each other's lives, and we knew just what the other would do or say in any circumstance. I knew what Jimmy was going to say before he said it.

'I hate this job. They don't pay us enough. We should take a machine-gun and get rid of all these no-good characters.'

Jimmy must have said that at least once a day. He was frustrated with his job and he made sure everybody knew about it.

One hot summer day we were out on patrol. The temperature was in the nineties and the atmosphere was thick. Because of the tall buildings and the traffic, New York City gets a lot of smog, and this day was so bad it made our eyes sting. We stood on a corner, trying to keep still, hoping a slight breeze might come along the street and cool us down.

Jimmy took his hat off and wiped his brow.

'Boy, it's hot,' he said. 'Why don't we try to find somewhere cooler?'

'Where we gonna find somewhere cool in this place?' I asked.

'I got an idea. Come with me.'

I followed Jimmy as he walked off down a side street. He went a few yards and then he stopped. I looked around – I couldn't see anywhere that might be cool – but Jimmy was bending down.

'Don't just stand there, help me,' he said. He was lifting a manhole cover.

'What you doing, Jimmy?' I said. 'Are you crazy?'

'Just trust me, okay?'

I sighed. We weren't going to go anyplace else until Jimmy had done whatever he wanted to do, so I bent over and between us we pulled off the manhole cover. Jimmy started to go down the steps. I shook my head.

'Why you going down there, Jimmy? What you thinking of?'

'Just follow me.'

I figured maybe the heat had gone to his head, but I couldn't leave him alone like that so I climbed down after him. There were about thirty steps that led down into the sewers. At the bottom, there were a table and some chairs, I guess for the workmen to take a break. Jimmy sat down, took off his gun belt and put his feet up.

'That's better,' he sighed.

It *was* cooler down there, and it was a relief just to take off all the heavy equipment we had to carry – gun, radio, cuffs – that always seemed to weigh more in the heat.

'Ain't that better?' Jimmy asked me.

'Yeah, Jimmy, you're right, it is.'

'Aw, man, I hate this job,' Jimmy was off. 'They don't pay us enough. I can't take these people. We oughta . . .'

He stopped talking and looked at me in surprise as I suddenly stood up.

'Jimmy, I don't hate this job,' I said. 'I don't care if they don't pay me enough. I love these people because I've got Jesus.'

Jimmy knew I was a Christian, but I'd never had the opportunity to tell him what Jesus meant to me because he just wasn't interested.

To my amazement, Jimmy's lip started to quiver and he began to cry.

'Mike, my son is only fourteen and he's already seeing a psychiatrist. My home is wrecked, I'm wrecked. What did you just say to me?'

'I don't know, I just spoke without thinking. What did I say to you?'

'Just think, Mike, it was something about Jesus.'

'Well, you're always saying these things to me 'bout how you hate everything, and I just said it back to you, but that I don't hate anyone because I got Jesus.'

'I'd love to be like that.'

At that moment it was like the whole sewer lit up, and God spoke into me saying, 'Today is Jimmy's day.' I grabbed his hand.

'Would you really like that, Jimmy? Do you want this hope?'

'Yeah, Mike, I do.'

So deep down under the streets in the bowels of New York City, Jimmy and I prayed and Jimmy's life was turned round. Many times after that Jimmy would say, to anyone who listened, not how much he hated his job but 'I got saved in the sewers of New York!'

The weekend, beginning with Friday evening, is the worst time to be a cop. Criminal activity increases roughly in relation to the amount of alcohol that is drunk, and cops are kept busy. And it's even worse if there's a full moon. There is something about such a night that brings out even more evildoers. On nights like that, when the moon is big and round in the sky, I don't need anyone to tell me 'there's gonna be trouble tonight'.

So it was a Friday night with a full moon and I was just about to take my meal-break. I walked into a restaurant and the owner spotted me and came rushing up.

'Officer, am I glad to see you. That fellow over there doesn't want to pay his bill.'

I looked at him. Was he serious? I couldn't believe that on a Friday night, one of the busiest nights of the week, he was worried just because someone refused to pay his bill.

'Look, sir, let me go and talk to him.'

'I want my money. You gotta make him pay up.'

I didn't want to arrest a guy on a weekend night just because he owed a few dollars. The guy the owner was complaining about was sitting quietly at a table by himself. He was wearing a short-sleeved shirt and he had thick muscular arms, the sort that the veins stand out on, but he didn't look that dangerous. I went over to him. I knew that everyone in the restaurant was pretending to eat while they were watching me, waiting to see what this cop was going to do.

I put my hands on the table and leaned over to the guy.

'The owner says you don't want to pay him, is that right?'

The guy nodded.

'Well, listen, the owner doesn't want to press charges but he does want his money. Why don't you just pay him?'

'Nuh-uh.'

'What about you and me going outside and talking about this?'

At that the guy stood up. He was a good head taller than me and built like the Incredible Hulk.

'I'm not p-p-paying nothing for the f-f-food. What y-y-you gonna do about it?'

What I'd have liked to have done was crawl under the

table, but I knew I couldn't back down now.

'C'mon please, let's us go outside. We can settle this peaceably out there.'

'I-I-I'm not going out there.'

The other diners, sensing that a fight was about to happen, began getting up and backing away from our table.

'C'mon, fella . . .'

With that he threw a punch. I ducked. I pulled out my nightstick and hit him with it. The stick broke clean in half. He stood there chuckling.

'W-w-what you g-g-gonna do now?'

My thought was, 'I w-w-wanna quit!'

But I had to act, so, without giving him time to think, I leapt at him and grabbed his throat. He kept taking swings at me but I was ducking and keeping my hands firmly in place. I had no intention of letting go until he had calmed down. The owner, meanwhile, had realised that things were getting out of hand and had called the precinct, and 'the troops' came to my rescue. With their help, I got the cuffs on and managed to bundle him into the squad car to take him to the precinct.

We walked in. The entrance was full of cops and their prisoners, all waiting to be booked. The sergeant on duty on the desk looked up, and when he saw us he groaned, 'Oh, no, no, Bobby, not you again!' Then to me he yelled, 'Get him out of here, psycho him, get him down to the hospital.'

'Oh, come on, Sarge, that will take hours. Can't you just book him here?'

'Our cells are full, he needs to be psycho'd, take him away . . . NOW!'

I turned and went back out to the car. I pushed Bobby in the back and got in the driver's seat.

'Okay, Bobby, you just sit there quiet. We got a long night ahead of us,' I warned him. I wasn't in the best of moods. I knew what was ahead of us.

At any time of the day or night Bellevue Hospital was busy; there were always people with problems waiting to be dealt with. When we arrived there was already a big queue. Some guys were handcuffed to chairs or railings, and others were standing around just talking to themselves. I gave Bobby's details to the nurse on reception, then we took our seats in the waiting room. Occasionally another person would walk past and snarl, 'What you looking at?' to which Bobby'd reply, 'W-w-what you looking at?' and I'd have to say, 'Sit down Bobby.'

Eventually our names were called.

'Officer DiSanza and Bobby Salermi.'

'That's us,' I said and we followed the nurse into the doctor's room. As soon as we got inside Bobby started, 'D-D-Doc, I'm not the g-g-guy you want to see.' He pointed at me with his head. 'H-h-he's the psycho.'

The doctor looked at me and back at Bobby.

'Okay, Bobby, we'll talk to him in a minute, but let's talk to you first.'

After listening to us both, the doctor said, 'Okay, Bobby, I'm going to give you some pills and I want you to promise me that you'll take them.'

'S-s-sure, D-D-Doc, I'll do as you s-s-say.'

'Is that it?' I said. 'Aren't you gonna keep him in?'

'Look, we've got homicidal maniacs here. We're full to bursting. There's no way I can keep him in, but the pills I'm going to give him should help.'

So at five o'clock in the morning, Bobby and I were back outside the hospital and I took off his handcuffs. You would never have known that just four hours previously I was fighting for my life. Bobby had sobered up now and was quiet and friendly. I was tired and fed up.

'W-w-well, Mike, w-w-what we gonna do now?'

'What are we gonna do now? We? You mean what are *you* gonna do now. I'm outta here.'

'But how do I get b-b-back to the Bronx?'

'Walk? Swim? I don't care. I'm going home to my bed.'

'B-b-but I can't go up that s-s-street. There's P-P-Puerto Ricans on that street. Th-th-they'll kill me.'

'That's your problem. You should have thought of that six hours ago.'

'B-b-but Mike, can't you g-g-give me a lift?'

I couldn't believe I was hearing this from the guy who a short while ago had fought me, but then the Holy Spirit spoke to me and said, 'Look, take a close look at this boy. He's a troubled kid, help him.'

I wanted to argue, 'Look I'm tired, it's been a long night, I want to go home to my bed. I don't want to have take this guy, who's caused me one problem after another tonight, any place,' but suddenly I realised Bobby was scared.

'Okay,' I said at last, 'I'll give you a lift, but if you make one wrong move we ain't wrestling this time, you get the picture?'

'Yeah, M-M-Mike, I don't want to get s-s-shot.'

So with Bobby in the back of the car, I drove back to the Bronx.

'C-c-can you drop me here, M-M-Mike? That's m-m-my uncle's restaurant.'

I stopped the car outside and an elderly Italian man came hurrying out.

'Where were you all night, Bobby? You been getting into trouble again?'

'N-n-no, uncle, it's all right. I was with my b-b-buddy Mike.'

The uncle looked at me.

'Officer, what happened?'

I explained about the restaurant and the trip to Bellevue, and then said, 'Do me a favour, get him out of here, and make sure he takes his pills, will you? I've done my bit for him.'

Bobby's uncle was very grateful to me. He knew that I could have made it hard for the whole family.

'Come in, Officer, come in and eat something before you

go. Let me thank you for all that you've done for Bobby.'

I knew that Bobby wasn't really a bad person, that he just had some problems, and sometimes he drank a bit too much and that made it all worse, but I was glad to get home after that long night.

But it wasn't that easy to get away from Bobby.

A couple of weeks later I was in the district when Frank, one of my fellow officers, came up to me.

'I met a cousin of yours the other day, Mikey.'

'Oh yeah, what was his name?' I had a lot of cousins all over the Bronx, so that wasn't unusual. Frank looked in his memobook where he'd written down my cousin's name.

'Let's see. Oh, yeah, that's right, it was Bobby Salermi.'

I groaned, 'Oh, no, he's not my cousin!'

Over the next month, at least ten cops must have come up to me and said the same thing. Bobby was telling everyone that 'Mikey's my cousin, Mikey's a great guy'.

From July 1976 through to 1977, there was a serial killer at work in New York City. He was known as the Son of Sam. Over a thirteen-month period, he killed six people and wounded another seven. It was a major investigation for the NYPD, and the newspapers were regularly full of articles about the killer, who he might be, his motives – and, especially, when were the police going to catch him? As the public's anxiety grew, the pressure on the force to find the killer became greater. Suspects were often brought in and questioned.

Because I mostly worked nights, I slept during the day. I'd wake at about four o'clock in the afternoon and Ann would have my dinner on the table. After we ate dinner, I'd watch the news on the television. One afternoon I switched the television on just as a special bulletin was broadcast. 'Police are today questioning a new suspect in the Son of Sam case. We're going over live now to the precinct.' And on to the television screen came a face I recognised. 'Police are holding Bobby Salermi for questioning.' As he was taken into the precinct, Bobby was struggling with the police officer holding him and furiously denying the charge. 'I'm not the S-S-Son of S-S-Sam. I may be a little crazy b-b-but I wouldn't k-k-kill people. You can ask my cousin Mike. He's a p-p-policeman.'

'Oh, no, Bobby, not you again.'

I stood up.

'What you doing, Mike?' Ann asked me.

'I gotta phone the precinct, I gotta explain.'

As it happened I didn't have time to call the precinct before the phone rang. Bobby had given the detectives my name and they wanted to interview me. I didn't believe Bobby was the Son of Sam, and when the detectives questioned me I did my best to convince them that he may have had a mental problem but he wasn't capable of the killings. Bobby was later released without charge, and eventually David Berkowitz was arrested and found guilty of the murders.

I saw Bobby a number of times after that and I often talked to him about Jesus. Then one day I said, 'Hey, Bobby, do you know Jesus loves you?'

'B-b-but of course, c-c-cos I know you love me and you love Jesus. I k-k-know you love Jesus cos you're always t-t-telling me about him.'

It was true, I had grown to love Bobby, and I had a real compassion for him. He wasn't a criminal, he just wasn't very bright, a hurting kid with mental problems. I grabbed his hand.

'Bobby,' I said, 'if I never see you again, I want to be sure that I'm gonna be with you for ever.'

'Mikey, you want to be my b-b-buddy in ever-ever-land?'

I'd told him before about heaven and now I told him again.

'If we die, and we love Jesus and have him as our saviour, then we go to heaven. That's where I'm going, Bobby, but I won't like it in heaven unless I know that you will be there too.'

'How do I get there?' Bobby looked at me with his big dark eyes.

I told him about the sinner's prayer and then said, 'Do you want this, Bobby?'

A big smile lit up his face.

'Yes, M-M-Mike, yes, I do.'

I took hold of his other hand.

'Now, Bobby, you've got to mean this. You mustn't say the words just to please me.'

'Tell me the story about J-J-Jesus again.'

So I told him about Jesus and how he'd died for us, and I explained everything as best I could to make sure he understood. Then I said, 'Now, Bobby, do you still want to ask Jesus to be your saviour?'

'Yes, M-M-Mike.'

'Okay, I'm going to pray and you say the words after me.'

After we'd finished the prayer, Bobby looked at me with his face glowing like an angel's and said, 'I f-f-feel so good, M-M-Mike.'

Later I suggested that he go to a church I knew, where they'd understand him and look after him, and he was soon settled in and feeling at home.

Bobby and I didn't meet under the best of circumstances, but now I thank God that he brought Bobby for a short period of time into my life.

Chapter 10

'Dillon?'

'Here, Sarge.'

'DiSanza?'

'Here, Sarge.'

'Ricardo?'

'Here, Sarge.'

It was early December and the desk sergeant was doing roll call at the start of our tour of duty. There were five of us in my squad waiting for our assignments for the night. On one side of me was Scotty Dillon and on the other were Marco, Micky and Ed.

In the time coming up to Christmas, when there was always an increase in criminal activity, it was important to know that the other guys you were working with could be relied on. These were all good cops and it was a pleasure to work with each of them. Ed was one of the few born-again Christians in the precinct and we'd shared some good times together, and Scotty and me went way back. We'd been buddies ever since our days in the police academy together.

Just a couple of nights after that roll call, Scotty was out on patrol. He answered a call to apprehend a man with a knife, and in the fight that ensued Scotty was badly cut about the face. The combination of the physical wound and the emotional stress resulted in him taking early retirement for health reasons. Scotty was glad to be out, and although I was pleased for him I was sad to see him go. Anyone in the police force or the army or, I guess, any occupation knows that when a colleague leaves, he'll always promise to keep in touch with the guys he's leaving behind, but the fact is very few people do. It's not that they don't want to or that they don't mean it when they say it, it's just that other things seem to become more important. So I figured that I wouldn't see Scotty again, and I was going to miss him.

Although the salary in the police force was good compared to some jobs, it still wasn't easy to raise a growing family on what we earned. I don't think that they paid us enough for what we did. Marco had three young children, and in order to earn some extra money to buy them the gifts they wanted for Christmas he started doing a second job in his spare time. When he wasn't on duty or grabbing a few hours' sleep, Marco drove a taxi-cab. It was a good job to have just before Christmas, when even more people than usual wanted to go out on the town. One night, just after Scotty's wounding, Marco was in the cab when he stopped to pick up a young guy. He didn't know it would be the last thing he'd do. The boy got in and shot Marco dead. For the small amount of money he had taken that night, Marco died at the hands of a sixteen-year-old thug.

It was a tremendous shock to all of us that one of our own should get shot, not on duty – that was bad enough – but as an innocent victim of crime. We all felt the sorrow, especially coming as it did a few days after the incident with Scotty. Micky was particularly close to Marco – they'd often worked as partners – and he felt it worse than anyone. He was finding it hard to do his police duty after Marco's death, so he decided to take a few days off and get away from it all. He drove up into Pennsylvania, in some of the worst weather of the winter, and in the middle of a storm his car ran out of gas. I don't know exactly what happened then, but for some reason he didn't stay in his car to wait for help. He must have figured that he knew where he was going and went off walking down the road. Micky was very much overweight and out of shape for a cop, and he must have sat down on a tree stump to take a rest. That was where they found him the next day, frozen to death.

When the news got back to the district, a deep sense of gloom descended on all of us. I thought back to that roll call just a couple of weeks earlier when there had been five of us in the line-up. Out of that five, one had retired injured and another two were dead. I knew God had promised to protect me, but that didn't stop me feeling sorrow and my heart was filled with a great sense of loneliness. I had seen so much, experienced so many tragedies over the years, I couldn't believe that I was still able to perform as a cop. And, of course, Ann felt it too. She heard of all these untimely deaths of cops, some she'd met, others where she knew their wives, and it all weighed heavy on her. She knew of God's promise to me, but she asked, as well, 'How long can this go on, Mike? How much more of this can we take?'

We knew Christmas that year would be hard. We knew we had to make the effort to be cheerful for the sake of our children, but as the big day approached it got harder and harder.

The night before Christmas Eve I was on duty as usual. I'd just been down to my locker to store my things, and I was on my way back up the stairs when I bumped into Ed coming down.

'Hi, Ed, how you doing?'

'Not too good, Mike. Can I talk to you?'

'Yeah, sure, Ed, I'll just go tell the sarge what I'm doing. I'll meet you in the coffee-shop in a minute.'

The guys often talked to me if they had problems. They knew that I wouldn't laugh or tell anyone what they said, and that I could be trusted to give them whatever help I could. The sergeant was an old buddy of mine and he understood the counselling role I sometimes played; when I explained to him that Ed wanted to talk, he said, 'Sure, Mike, take your time.'

Downstairs I found Ed staring into a large cup of coffee. He was stirring it round and round. I got myself a cup and sat down with him. I let him talk and he shared with me some of the problems he'd been having.

'And as if that's not enough, Micky and Marco go and get killed and Christmas is coming and, Mike, I'm so depressed, I don't know what to do with myself.'

I didn't really have any answers for him so I did what I always do in those circumstances.

'Look Ed, I do know how you're feeling and I understand a bit of what you're going through. I wish I could make it all right for you, but I can't. But we both know someone who can, don't we?'

Ed looked at me, desperation written all over his face.

'Let's pray together, Ed,' I said, 'here and now, let's ask Jesus to help you.'

And on that night, 23rd December, Ed and I sat at the table in the coffee-shop and prayed. When we'd finished, I said, 'Ed, you're not well, you've been under pressure. Why don't you take a few days off sick?'

'No, Mike, it's okay. Talking with you has helped, it's made me get things into perspective a little. I feel better just for this.'

His face looked less anxious and I left him, hoping that things would start to improve for him. I went back to my duties and finished my tour as usual. I went home, got some sleep, helped Ann with the last-minute preparations, and before I knew it, it was getting close for me to leave for the midnight shift and my Christmas Eve tour of duty.

As soon as I walked into the precinct I knew something was wrong. Everything was very quiet, and that was unusual for any night, let alone a night before Christmas. There were a couple of guys in there sitting at desks, doing paperwork, and another couple just sitting around, their heads bent. I knew something had happened. I'd seen this behaviour before. I walked up to the desk as the sergeant was just coming out of the office, his face solemn.

'Hey, Sarge, what happened?'

'We got a call two hours ago. Ed committed suicide in front of his building. He shot himself in the head.'

'Oh no,' I doubled over. 'Oh, Lord, no.'

These weren't only cops that I had worked with, they were my buddies. Of the five of us in the early December roll call, I was the only one left in my squad, and I didn't know how much more I could take. I really felt as if I might have a nervous breakdown. The grief was just too much.

There are many Christmas incidents that stand out in my memory for different reasons.

Another time, several years before, I had an earlier than usual tour of duty on Christmas Eve. I was due to finish at midnight. It was a freezing cold night, we were in the middle of a big blizzard and there were ten inches of snow on the ground. At roll call I was given my tour of duty – I had to patrol from 125th to 138th Street – and I figured it was okay. Even allowing for the weather and battling through the snow, I should be able to be home by one o'clock in the morning. All I could think of was being home for Christmas with my family, but God had other ideas.

I was physically warm because I was wrapped up snug in my winter gear and I had that great warmth in my heart that comes from knowing Jesus, but as I walked on my patrol and looked around me, I felt a chill. On those streets in Harlem and the South Bronx it didn't look like Christmas at all. There were no decorations or bright lights to be seen, none of the things we associate with Christmas, just buildings – some of them derelict and abandoned – garbage mixed with snow in the streets, and people coming out of bars and late-night grocery stores. Even though the sight didn't look like Christmas, I thanked Jesus because he had given me peace in my heart.

I felt very close to Jesus. I shared everything with him. I didn't have to go through a priest or anyone else when I wanted to talk to him; I talked to him like the best buddy he was. All the time on patrol, I'd be talking to him, saying, 'Oh, Lord, just look at that,' or, 'Will you look at this, so much pain, Lord,' or, 'Will you help me here, Lord?' I saw so many tragic sights: it was only being able to share it with Jesus, knowing he understood how I felt and how the people around me felt, that I was able to deal with them. But even then depression continued to plague me. Seeing death, violence and sadness every day is wearing, and it brought me down.

At about 9.30 that evening I saw a silhouette of a man beside a lamp-post. I approached him carefully, but when I got closer I could see that he was hanging on to the lamp-post. He was freezing cold and badly injured. Blood was dripping from one eye. He was a black boy, about eighteen years old. He had bare feet and he held out his arm to me, saying in a quiet hoarse voice, 'Help me.'

'Okay, brother, you're gonna be all right,' I said, and I called up on my radio for an ambulance.

'Sorry, Officer,' the voice on the other end of my radio said, 'the ambulances can't get out of the garage, the snow's too thick. They're trying to clear it now but it will be a while before they can get to you.'

'Oh, no. This kid's in real trouble, he needs to go to a hospital.'

'I'm sorry, Officer, the ambulance will get to you as soon as it can, but I don't know when that will be.'

I looked at the boy. I couldn't leave him there but I didn't know what to do with him. I looked around, and then I remembered there was a restaurant just down the block. If I could get him there at least it would warm him up some. I put my arm under his and around his back and gripped his other side.

'C'mon, brother, let's get you down to the restaurant. Just lean on me. I can take most of your weight if you can just move your legs.'

The boy was just about numb with the cold but he managed to push one leg in front of the other.

'That's right, you can do it,' I said, and slowly we made our way to the restaurant. I kicked the door open and we fell into the brightly lit warm room. Seeing us stumble in, one of the workers rushed over to help me get the boy on to a chair.

'Here, you sit down here, and you too, Officer. I'll go get some nice hot soup for you both.'

I sat back on my chair, catching my breath, and then I looked at the young man again. Now, in the light, I could see him more clearly. His hair was in an Afro style, and the few clothes he wore were stained and torn. He had a deep cut across his cheek from the corner of his eye and blood from it had dried on his face and his jacket. His hands were bruised black and blue, and mucus was running out of his nose down his chin on to his chest. People sitting at the other tables were staring at him and at me.

The nearest hospital, St Mary's, was a mile away: I couldn't carry him that far. I tried on my radio again to see if the ambulances were on the move yet, but the work to clear the roads was still going on. I didn't know what to do. I couldn't leave him, not in his condition. I had to wait with him.

The man brought over our bowls of steaming hot soup,

and I picked up my spoon and began to eat.

'Hey, this is good,' I said, and then I looked at the young man. He wasn't touching his.

'What's the matter?' I asked. 'The soup's good, taste some.'

He still didn't move, and suddenly I realised that he couldn't. It wasn't that he didn't want to, but his hand was too frozen and numb to pick up the spoon. And then the Holy Spirit spoke to me. He said, 'Help him.'

'Naah.'

I wasn't entertaining that. I was horrified at the suggestion. People were already staring at us – I didn't want to make even more of an exhibition of myself.

'Go on, help him.'

'But Lord, what will all these people think?'

'Stop worrying about what people think! Do as I ask you.'

'Okay, Lord, I'll do as you ask.'

I picked up the boy's spoon, dipped it into the soup and lifted it to my mouth. I blew on it to cool it down a bit and then put the spoon to his mouth. He sipped eagerly, and I felt so good. I really didn't care any more what the other people in the restaurant thought. I was discovering what a wonderful feeling it was to give of myself and allow God to work through me.

Soon after that a police emergency van pulled up outside the restaurant. They'd heard my call for help, and as the ambulances were still out of action they took me and the young man to St Mary's hospital. We got him inside, and I waited until he was attended to and his treatment started before I said goodnight to him and headed off for home.

It was three o'clock on Christmas morning by the time I finally got home. Ann was waiting up for me, and she'd prepared a meal for us to eat. We sat down at the table, which had a little Christmas tree on it, and gave thanks. I told Ann what had happened the previous evening and why I'd been late.

'D'you know, Ann,' I said, 'God did a great thing tonight. All over the world people are searching for some meaning to life. They're searching in bars, in drugs, in immorality, but here tonight, on a desolate street in the middle of the South Bronx, God made himself known. He worked through me to help another human being. God is so good.'

Later on Christmas Day, when we'd had some sleep, Ann said to me, 'What we gonna do today? Your mom wants us to go over to her house.'

'Okay,' I said, 'but before we go I want to visit that young man I took into hospital last night.'

I took the subway over to St Mary's and asked the nurse at the reception desk where I would find him. She pointed me in the right direction and I headed off there. He was in a room by himself, and when I arrived he was asleep. He had tubes plugged into him everywhere and he looked very young and helpless. I waited for a while to see if he'd wake, but he didn't so I left and went over to my parents' place, where I was meeting Ann and the kids.

The next day I felt God tell me to go and see the young man again, so I set off, arrived at the hospital and found him asleep.

The third day when God told me to go and see the young man I wasn't too happy.

'Lord, you keep telling me to go and see him and he's always asleep. What is the point in that?'

'Just go.'

As far as the young man was concerned, the police had no further interest in him. But God had. So I went off again. This time he was sitting up in bed.

'How you doing?' I said.

'Who are you, man?'

'I'm the guy who brought you in here.'

'You didn't bring me in here – they told me a cop brought me in here.'

'Yeah, I'm the cop.'

'You ain't no cop.'

'You know your problem: you talk too much!'

I was fed up. I'd made the effort for three days, over the Christmas period when I should have been enjoying myself with my family, to take the time to go and visit him, and this was the thanks I was getting. But God said, 'Whoa, remember that sick young man you brought in? He needs to know something and I want you to tell him.'

I sat down and I started talking to the young man. I hadn't been a Christian that long, but I knew God wanted me here for a reason. I told him a little of my story, how I'd grown up in the Bronx and how I'd met Jesus. Then I said, 'I don't know what it's all about, I'm still learning myself, but I do know that God loves you and that he sent me here to tell you that.'

I didn't know how to preach, I just knew that God wanted me to help this guy. I gave him a New Testament and a small pamphlet that explained things a little better than I could.

'Brother,' I said, 'if you let Jesus into your heart, he can change your life.'

Then I left.

I didn't go into the hospital again. I was real busy working and being with my family for the holiday period, and I didn't have any spare time. Anyway I'd said all that I had to, and as the days passed I soon forgot about him.

Two years later I was out on patrol when a bus pulled up alongside me. I was outside a Baptist church – nearly every street corner in Harlem has some sort of church on it – and the people getting off the bus were all going into the building. They were friendly and polite, greeting me, the local neighbourhood cop.

'How you doing, Officer?'

'Have a nice day.'

'God bless you, Officer.'

I was happy to stand a moment and exchange words when suddenly someone came up behind me, grabbed my shoulders and kissed me on the cheek. It didn't faze me, being kissed on the cheek; nothing in New York fazed me any more.

I turned round and saw a black young man and an older man, both in suits, white shirts and neat ties, standing there. The younger man was grinning at me.

'Hey, Pastor,' he said to the other man, 'you remember my story 'bout how I got saved?'

The pastor began to smile, 'I remember.'

'I told you how, two years ago at Christmas, a policeman took me to hospital and gave me a Bible.'

'You told me.'

'And he fed me with soup because I was too frozen to pick up my spoon.'

'I remember. And now you've found your policeman friend?'

'Yeah. Do you remember me, Officer?'

Slowly I began to remember, and I nodded as I recalled our first meeting. I was amazed. The last time I had seen him had been in the hospital, destitute and ill, but now standing before me was this smartly dressed, healthy-looking kid.

'Wow, is it really you?' I said. 'What happened to you?'

'I read the tract and then I started reading the Bible you gave me, and I got saved. I went to Bible College in Alabama to learn more about Jesus.'

'So what you doing here in New York?'

'At the end of Bible College, I asked God what I should do now and he said, "Go back to where you started and give the precious gospel to the people of New York." So here I am.'

'Okay, brother,' I grinned, 'you take this side of town and I'll take the other!'

People came in and out of my life all the time. Sometimes the reason for it was obvious; other times I never knew why I'd met someone or what had happened to them. This time I was allowed to know, and I praised God for his mighty work and the way he lets me help him in it.

Chapter 11

The Christmas season is always a busy time for the police. For some people it can be a time of deepening depression – if things aren't going good in your own personal life, the joy of Christmas can bring you down – and suicide rates increase at Christmas and the New Year. With all of the parties going on there seems to be an increase in drunkenness and crime, and it all adds up to making a cop's life harder. But even with many difficult situations there was always plenty to be joyful about.

One Christmas Eve, Jimmy and I were on patrol in Manhattan. We were both excited, looking forward to getting off work and enjoying the festivities with our families. Manhattan was jam-packed with thousands of people rushing around, some doing last-minute shopping, many visiting the city to see the lights and the decorations. As we drove down to the Rockefeller Center in the patrol car, we put the light to go round. We waved and shouted, 'Merry Christmas,' and many people, especially the kids, waved and shouted it back at us. We drove past the ice-skating rink and pulled up close to the famous Christmas tree outside the Center. We could see people were wondering what was going on, wondering if there was trouble somewhere. Jimmy and I both got out of the car and walked right up next to the tree. Then, on the count of three, we yelled together, 'Happy Birthday, Jesus!' People all around us started cheering and laughing and clapping. We must have stayed there for about two hours, just talking to people about Christmas and about Jesus if they were interested. It's not often that being a cop brings such a good feeling, and it was great being able to share it with Jimmy.

Another time I had to work from midnight on Christmas Eve to eight o'clock on Christmas morning. It was a bitterly cold night – it must have been well below freezing to begin with, but the wind made it feel even colder. My assignment for the night was to ride the 'A' train from 125th Street to Howard Beach.

At about a quarter after one we pulled into one of the further stations on the route and a voice came over the loudspeaker.

'All passengers please leave the train. The signals ahead are frozen and the train cannot go any further.'

The signals were frozen on red against us, and trains are not allowed to go through red lights under any circumstances. About fifty people got off the train. We all knew they would have to wait at least twenty minutes for the next train, and it wasn't like the subway – here the station was in the open air and there was very little shelter. Several of the passengers made their way to the token clerk's booth and began complaining and demanding their money back. Some of them started banging on the booth and I could see there was danger of a riot starting.

I didn't want to radio in for assistance because I didn't want to escalate the situation. I was taking a chance, but experience told me to wait a while.

Twenty-five minutes later another train pulled in. And just after that, another one. The signals were still frozen, and the passengers were very unhappy at being turned out into the cold. There must have been a hundred and fifty people standing on the mezzanine now, some with children, many yelling and shouting, and they knew they were in for a long wait. The area we were in was part of the city, but more suburban. There were no cabs around, and even if there had been there wouldn't have been enough for everyone – anyway, most of the passengers riding the train wouldn't have been able to afford the high prices they'd have been charged.

I heard someone shout, 'Let's overturn the booth and take the money,' and I realised I had to do something quick. I was the sole police officer in the middle of an angry crowd, and there was no way I could take control on my own. I bowed my head and asked Jesus, 'Lord, how am I gonna get out of this one?'

I felt the Holy Spirit say to me, 'Why don't you ask them to sing a song?'

I looked around at the crowd. I knew most of them would have had some religious upbringing, so I figured I'd give it a try.

'Listen up, people,' I shouted. 'Look, you guys and gals outnumber me. I didn't ask this train to stop and I don't want to be here any more than you do. I'd rather be home with my family. I'm not your enemy – matter of fact, about Christmas we most probably all believe in the same thing. We'll see if we can get some coffee going, but meantime let's try and make the best of this. I'm gonna sing a song. Why don't you join in with me?'

'Silent night, holy night,' I started to sing. I'm not a great singer, but soon a few of the ladies joined in and then, after two or three verses, I could hear some deeper voices adding to the chorus. We sang the carol through a couple of times, and soon even the ones who'd been agitating the crowd had calmed down and were listening quietly. While we were singing, yet another train pulled in, and people getting off heard us and wondered what was happening.

In the open air, our voices rose and were carried out far into the night. I was transported, and in my spirit I felt as if heaven and earth were one. The singing was just beautiful. For those few minutes I didn't even feel the cold. I never felt such peace in all of my life. The peace that passes all understanding.

Meanwhile, down in the despatch room they'd made coffee and they brought it round for all of us. There were a few heaters, and I made sure that all the women and children got up close to those. The atmosphere was better now, and people were drinking their coffee and talking with one another.

At last, at about four o'clock on Christmas morning, the voice came over the loudspeaker again.

'The signal has been fixed.'

A cheer went up from the crowd.

'The next train, which will be arriving in two minutes, will take all of you to your destinations.'

Another cheer from the crowd. People started picking up their bags and getting themselves ready. The train pulled into the station and all the passengers piled on to it. I stood by one of the open doors and wished everyone a good night and a merry Christmas. One by one, as they streamed past me, they acknowledged my greeting or gave me a 'high five', and said, 'Thank you, brother.'

Their response meant a lot to me. I was a white policeman in amongst a black and Hispanic crowd who'd been kept waiting for a long time in extremely unpleasant conditions. Things could very easily have turned nasty – but I'd found out once again that the love of God is enough to cover a multitude of problems.

The doors shut, the train pulled away, and I was left standing alone on the platform. I'd been anxious and afraid during the situation, and I'd taken a chance not calling for back-up. A riot could have broken out, many people could have been injured, and I could have been killed. In the silence of the night I stood in awe of God, who'd brought peace and calm where there could have been chaos.

At about 5.30 a.m. Richard turned up to take over from me. I wasn't expecting to be relieved until 7.00, but Richard, who was Jewish, knew the importance of this holiday to my religion, and he'd come early to give me more time to spend with my family. I really appreciated that, and I said, 'Richard, you'll never believe what's happened here tonight!'

He threw his arms in the air.

'I don't want to know what happened here tonight.'

I understood his attitude: he'd come in early as a favour and he didn't want to know about any trouble there'd been. But I was persistent. I told him, and he was amazed when he heard my story. He said, 'Mike, that is hard for me to believe. It's such a cold night, and it's a holiday time. People would have wanted to get home and they were stuck for three hours on this station – that should have been cause for a riot.'

Just then the token clerk came running out of his booth. He'd barricaded himself in when it had looked like there was going to be trouble, and he'd stayed in there all night. Now he pointed at me and said, 'This cop should get a medal of honour for saving my life!'

Richard shook his head as he realised the truth of my story and he said, 'I guess this was a Christmas miracle for you, Mike.'

I went back to the district, changed my clothes, got into my own car and drove home. Ann and I had a young family now, and I knew the kids would be up already and waiting for me, all excited, wanting to open their presents. As I drove I thought, 'I must be the most blessed man this Christmas to be able to experience the power of God in a situation that could have cost my life.'

I could hear my children as I pulled into the driveway! They were looking out of the window.

'Here comes Daddy, here he is!'

I walked in the door to be greeted by Ann, the kids and my mom and dad, who were staying with us. Ann said, 'Hi, honey, merry Christmas. Come on, sit down here, I'll make you a hot drink to warm you up.'

Every year Ann made her famous Irish Christmas pudding, full of nuts and fruit and cherries, and she gave me a slice of that along with a mug of steaming hot chocolate. I sat at the kitchen table, took one sip, my head dropped and I fell fast asleep. The cold and the high anxiety I'd felt during the night had combined to make me very tired. My family understood and my dad helped me to get upstairs to bed.

'Don't worry, Mike,' Ann said, 'we'll have Christmas when you wake up.'

One of the things policemen's families have to get used to through the years is the fact that the holiday season is a busy time for police and there's very little leave allowed. While everyone else gets time off, cops have to work harder than ever. So it wasn't too much of a surprise on roll call one night in early December when the sergeant on duty, the Irish sergeant that I'd met on my very first day, said, 'Nobody will put in for leave for Christmas Eve or Christmas Day. All available men are needed to work.'

We all accepted it. It was the same every year; it was just the way things were. There was no use complaining.

Ann loves Christmas; it's her favourite season. As soon as the calendar changes to 1st December, she starts baking: cake, puddings, cookies, meals to freeze ahead ready to share with others. This particular year, though, I noticed that she didn't seem to have the same enthusiasm; in fact she seemed a little depressed. That wasn't like her at all.

I was about to go off to work one night in the middle of December when I saw Ann sitting on her chair, just staring into space. I said, 'Ann, are you okay? You don't seem yourself.'

She looked up at me and I was shocked to see the weariness in her face.

She said, 'Mike, do you know that you haven't had a Christmas off in over ten years? Can you please try to get it off this year?'

By her voice I could tell that she was desperate. I remembered what the sergeant had said and I knew it was no use, but I didn't want to say that.

'I don't know, Ann,' I said, 'you know what it's like, how busy we always are.'

She groaned, 'Can't you just try, Mike?'

'Okay, honey, I'll try,' I said, 'but let's pray about it, shall we?'

We went outside on to the driveway and looked up at the clear starry sky. We held hands and I prayed, 'Dear God, in Jesus' name, can you please let us get Christmas off?'

When we'd finished, I kissed Ann goodbye and went off to work. I didn't feel any confidence or assurance that God would answer this prayer; rather, I felt a void. It didn't seem to me that God could even hear my prayer.

I got to work, changed into my uniform, filled out the form to apply for leave, and put it in.

The next night when I arrived for work the sergeant called me over to the desk.

'Hey, DiSanza, come here.'

I went over. He gave me back my form.

'Heh?' was all he said, but I knew what he meant: what are you doing asking for leave when I've already told you can't have it? Written across my form in big red letters was the single word: DISAPPROVED.

I did my tour of duty and went home, dreading telling Ann. She came hurrying up to meet me.

'How did the request for leave turn out?' she asked.

I didn't say anything, just got the piece of paper out of my pocket and showed her.

'Oh, no.'

'Hey, don't give up, we prayed about it, remember? It's not Christmas Eve yet. Let's wait and see what happens.'

I came home at breakfast time on 23rd December and Ann said, 'Anything happen? They change their mind and give you the day off?'

I shook my head. Ann was real upset now.

'Well, I'm gonna call that sergeant and tell him you deserve a day off. You haven't had a Christmas off for years and I'm gonna tell him I want you to have time off.'

Ann knew that she wouldn't really call the district – apart from anything else, I would be real embarrassed if the guys found out my wife had been on the phone demanding time off for me – but she was just so upset.

'It's still not Christmas Eve yet,' I said. 'Let's wait and see.'

I went to work that night as usual. I was on patrol in the subway when I heard a report on the radio that a woman had had her pocketbook – bag – snatched. The suspect was male, about five feet eleven inches tall, thin and wearing a maroon sweater. He'd last been seen running in the direction of 96th Street. It was in my area, so I figured I'd check out some of the trains in case he'd tried to make his getaway on them. I checked a couple of trains, then went up on to the street and inspected a few buses. New York is crowded and busy at any time of day or night and especially just before Christmas, but there was no sign of the suspect. I saw a few guys who fitted the description, but none of them was wearing a maroon sweater.

I went back down into the subway and got on another train. I looked around and I spotted a guy sitting in the corner seat. He was avoiding my eyes and he looked nervous. He almost fitted the description, except he was wearing a green sweater. I was about to give up and get off when I noticed that the inside of the cuff of his sweater was maroon. I decided it was worth checking out. I walked over to him.

'Excuse me, sir,' I said, 'could I see the inside of your sweater?'

'Hey, what you want? You picking on me?' He turned to the other passengers. 'See this cop? He's picking on me, it ain't right. Are you gonna help me?'

The other passengers on the train that night weren't interested in his plight, and as soon as he tried to get away I grabbed him, pulled up his sleeve and saw that it was a reversible sweater. Those were reasonable grounds to apprehend him and I took him into the precinct.

The lady whose pocketbook had been snatched came in and did a positive identification on him, and some of her belongings were found in his pocket. It wasn't a big arrest, but any apprehension is good. As I was doing the paperwork, the lieutenant of the district called to congratulate me on the arrest. 'Good job, Officer,' he said.

About twenty minutes later I had another call, this time from a detective. It turned out that the man I'd brought in was wanted in connection with a whole load of other felonies. Soon after that the duty captain called me. He had a strong Irish brogue. He said, 'Officer, dat was a foine job yah did for us. Is dere any-ting we can do for yah?'

'No, Captain, I was just doing . . .' I began, but suddenly it was like a light-bulb flashed on in my head. 'Well, perhaps I could run this by you, Captain.'

I hesitated. 'Are you from Ireland, Captain?'

'I am, yes.'

'My wife, Ann, is from Ireland too.'

'Is she now, and where is she from?'

'Dublin.'

'Ah, dat's a great city.'

'You know, Captain, my wife is a bit depressed this Christmas.'

'Arh, yah're not having nothing like a divorce, now are yah? We've enough of that in this department.'

'No, Captain, nothing like that, it's just that I've had to work for so many Christmases and she'd really like to have me home this year for a change.'

There was a moment's silence before the captain spoke again.

'Officer, can yah ask me some-ting else, ask me any-ting but dat? I don't tink I can do dat.'

'There's nothing else, Captain.'

He sighed.

'Call me back in half an hour. I'll see what I can do.'

I kept my eye on the clock as the hands slowly moved round, and exactly half an hour later I called him back.

'Officer DiSanza, have yah finished yahr paperwork?'

'Yes, I have.'

'Have yah arraigned yahr prisoner?'

'Yes, I have.'

'Then tell yahr Annie to have a wonderful Christmas – yah'll be home with her.'

I could hardly believe my ears.

'Thank you, Captain.'

'There'll be someone dere to relieve yah shortly, and we'll see yah back on the 26th.'

'Thank you, Captain.'

I fairly flew out of the district before they changed their minds and I arrived home at six o'clock on Christmas Eve morning. I didn't usually get home till much later, and Ann was still asleep. I went up and sat on the edge of the bed.

'Ann,' I said, 'guess what?'

She opened her eyes, saw me and yawned.

'Oh, is it nine o'clock already?'

'No, it's only six.'

'What are you doing here, then?'

'Ann, I got Christmas off!'

Ann sprang up in bed and her first words were, 'Oh, thank you, Jesus.'

We hugged each other and I told her what had happened to make it possible.

'So,' she said, 'the sergeant said DISAPPROVED, did he?'

'Yeah,' I joined in, 'but heaven said APPROVED!'

Chapter 12

'Mike, come over here, will you?'

The sergeant on the desk gestured me over to him. I'd just returned to the district from a softball game. I played on a team in the police league and we'd won our game that afternoon, so I was feeling good.

'Yeah, Sarge, what is it?'

'Mikey,' he said, 'there's been a phone call for you. Ann's not well. She's been taken to hospital.'

It was during the summer and Ann had been leading a vacation Bible Club. It was something she did every year. We now had four children – Michael, Douglas, Rachel and Jonathan – and we'd moved into a small house on Long Island. Each summer for one week Ann would organise this vacation Bible Club in our back-yard. She'd have maybe a hundred children between the ages of five and ten out there. With the aid of about ten helpers, Ann would get the children doing arts and crafts, playing games and singing, and reading Bible stories. At the end of each week there'd be a mini-graduation ceremony where the parents would be invited to see what their children had been doing during the week. There'd be certificates handed out and, at the end, an opportunity to share the gospel with the grown-ups. Over the years a number of parents and children accepted Christ as their saviour or renewed their faith. The Bible Club was a large part of Ann's ministry.

When I got the message I rushed off to the hospital and found Ann in a bed in a ward.

'Ann, honey, what happened to you?' I said.

'Mike, I don't know. One minute I was fine and then my leg went numb and I collapsed. I thought at first that it was just a muscle spasm and I got Linda to help me sit down, but after about half an hour I couldn't move my legs at all. Then Trish brought me here.'

They did some tests on Ann, and later the doctor came and told us that they believed that she had multiple sclerosis or MS, as it's known. We asked for a second opinion; another consultant examined her, did more tests, and he said the same thing. Ann had MS.

It came as a great shock to us. She was only in her early thirties. We had four children under ten, and I had a very busy ministry with Cops for Christ as well as my police work. We didn't know a lot about MS then but we knew it was serious. We started to read up on it and discovered just how serious it could be, often crippling people and sometimes leading to early death.

Her illness meant Ann was often confined to bed. There would be days when she was unable to drive or do anything around the house. I had to take on a lot of her chores. Cleaning the house, especially any heavy stuff, became my responsibility. Michael and Douglas were in school now, and each of the children were involved in different clubs and activities they needed to be taken to after school.

I knew I needed to be in top physical condition to deal with the extra workload, and I took up jogging. I'd jog for three or four miles at least five days a week, a habit I kept going for about twenty years. No matter what the weather was like in

New York, I'd jog. The roads were often empty when I jogged and I was able to spend the time communicating with God, meditating on his word and talking to him. I asked him, 'How can this have happened to us when we're doing so much for you?'

I know that some people believe that all sickness is the result of sin, but I believed that Ann's sickness came from the enemy, who resented the ministry we were doing. But I also knew that God was greater. 'The one who is in you is greater than the one who is in the world' (1 John 4:4).

I offered my prayer for healing for Ann up to the Lord and left it with him. I didn't know if he would heal her supernaturally, or gradually, or even if he would heal her at all, but I put it in his hands.

MS is a progressive disease, but sometimes there were periods when Ann's condition didn't deteriorate. She didn't get better, but she didn't get worse, either. She would have good times and bad times. Maybe she'd have two or three days when she felt okay and she'd be able to help around the house, and then all her energy would be drained from her and she wouldn't be able to get out of bed again for a week. The children were a great help during this time. Michael would cut the lawn, and Rachel learned early to be a housekeeper to help Mom. They never gave us any problems while Ann was sick.

We joined the MS Society and received and read their magazine each month. We wanted to find out all we could about the disease, and it was good to be in contact with others who were going through the same pain and emotional upset that we were.

We were also learning a lot about the Lord. We realised that Ann's illness was a cross that we would have to bear, and that we were to trust him in all things. It doesn't matter how much a person is doing for the Lord, tragedy can still happen, and we need to trust the Lord in that. The Bible says that 'My grace is sufficient for you, for my power is made perfect in weakness' (2 Corinthians 12:9). We were learning the truth of those words.

I didn't want Ann to feel guilty that she was sick and not able to help with the ministry so much, and I tried to always encourage her. Sometimes it was difficult when I wanted so desperately to see her healed.

I saw her suffer so much. On bad days parts of her body would go into a shaking spasm. As a policeman I'd seen human bodies physically mangled, I'd seen people in all kinds of emotional, physical and spiritual turmoil, but when it came to my own wife I was no good at dealing with it. Instead of comforting her, there were times when I just had to walk out of the room, because I couldn't watch her suffer any more and I didn't know how to deal with it. I'd perhaps go outside and pray and then go back into her room later and pray with her.

One evening about 6.30, Ann came into the room where I was watching the news on television. She said, 'Mike, can I ask you something?'

'Sure,' I said, 'what is it?'

'Can you get the night off tonight?'

I was due to go on duty at midnight, and changing duties, especially at short notice, was almost impossible because the roll calls were made up early.

'I doubt it, Ann, you know what it's like trying to get an excusal. Why do you want me home, anyway?'

'There's a man with a healing ministry coming to the church tonight; his name's Billy Burke. I feel the Lord wants me to be at this meeting, but I need you to be here to take care of the children.'

'Aw, it's such short notice, I really don't think I'll be able to.'

I looked at her face and I could see how much she wanted to go to this meeting.

'Okay, I'll give it a try,' I said. 'Just asking can't do any harm, can it?'

I called up the precinct, expecting the sergeant to answer

the phone, but instead it was the duty captain. He was a friend of mine and Ann's and he was part of Cops for Christ. I told him what I wanted.

'I know it's short notice, Captain John,' I said, 'but Ann believes it's God's will for her to be at this meeting tonight.'

'Don't worry, Mike,' he said, 'you got it. Tell Ann to go to the meeting.'

I came off the phone and told Ann I'd spoken to Captain John and that it was okay for me to stay at home that evening. As soon as I mentioned the captain's name, Ann's face lit up. She believed then that even that was part of God's plan for her healing.

Her friend Janet was driving her to the meeting. Before she went, Ann said to me, 'You know, Mike, even if this healer doesn't have the faith to believe for my healing, I do. I believe that God is going to heal me tonight.'

I said, 'That's good, honey,' and kissed her goodbye.

Ann's illness had taken its toll on her and me. Even though she was so confident, I didn't get too excited. I thought that maybe she would get healed, but could we really be that blessed? Jesus tells us to put all our cares on him, so I prayed for healing for Ann and left it at that.

When Ann came home from the meeting, she was real happy. She had gone up and joined the prayer line for healing, and Billy Burke had prayed over her and asked the Lord to heal her MS.

'And then, Mike, I felt a warmth come over my body. I dug deep into my faith and I asked God to heal me, and I believe he has, Mike. I don't think that I ever need worry about the effects of MS on my body again.'

Ever since that day Ann has functioned more or less normally. She gets tired sometimes and needs to rest, but she has never had to spend a single day in bed because of the MS.

Ann wasn't superfanatical in her prayer, she just had the

faith to believe and her faith motivated God's power. I was so happy for her.

Some years later I came home from work one morning and found Ann sitting crying at the kitchen table.

'What's the matter, Ann? Has something happened? Are the kids okay?'

Ann took out a tissue and blew her nose.

'They're fine and I'm okay now,' she said, 'it's just that I heard on the radio a while ago that a New York policeman had been shot and killed in the line of duty, and I couldn't get in touch with you, and I didn't know if it was you or not, and then when I found out it wasn't you I felt so sorry for the dead officer's wife.'

'Oh, Ann, honey.'

I hugged her to me, and the full impact of what she had gone through for years hit me. It wasn't just the wondering if I would come home safe each day. It was putting up with long hours, unsociable hours, having to work holidays. When there was a family function it was always difficult for us to get there. My vacation time was never in the summer, always in January and February, and with four children it was too expensive for us to go to Florida or anywhere sunny. And my ministry with Cops for Christ took me away from home a lot.

Ann put up with it all. She has always been a blessing to me. When God gave me my ministry, he made certain I had a helpmate who knew that my calling was sure and who understood and would stand by me. God gave me Ann, and gave her the grace to deal with everything that came our way. I thank her with my whole heart for being faithful.

Chapter 13

Over the course of my career, God stayed true to his word to help and protect me. When new cops joined the force they would soon hear from the others about Mikey Di and Jesus, and I could see from the way they looked at me that they didn't want to work with me – they were afraid that I wouldn't be tough enough or that they wouldn't be able to depend on me in an emergency. They soon learned that it was just the opposite, and cops would ask to be my partner on dangerous assignments because they realised that I had some kind of special protection.

Knowing that God was with me on the subways and the streets and that the Holy Spirit was looking out for me helped build my confidence in my ability to do the job. The gift of a heavenly language, or speaking in tongues as it's called in the Bible, is precious. The Holy Spirit would often warn me of trouble coming by telling me to pray in tongues. At 2.30 a.m., driving round the streets of Harlem, the Holy Spirit would sometimes tell me to stop the car and pray in the heavenly language. I'd get out and walk round the car praying until I felt a sense of peace. God gives the gift of tongues to believers to strengthen and build them up (1 Corinthians 14:4). I needed strengthening at certain times in my career – like every night! I needed to have my spirit lifted up constantly just to have the confidence to walk the streets and subways in the darkness, knowing that thousands of people out there were the victims of violence and oppression, and that their hatred could be turned against me at any time. I had to be prepared for anything. I know that some people don't believe in the gift of tongues, but on the beat in Harlem I found it to be a very real blessing.

I was on patrol one night when a message came over the radio that a policeman was in trouble in the subway station at Broadway in Manhattan. It was close by, so I responded to the call. I made my way there, praying all the way, 'Jesus, watch over me.'

When I arrived at the subway station, I ran down the steps to the platform. I heard the trouble before I saw it, the sounds of raised voices echoing up the steps. Ahead of me I saw a crowd of people jostling and pushing each other. In the midst of them was a cop. He was injured, and I could see he was struggling to handcuff one guy who was mouthing off and resisting arrest. At that time of night, some of the people you find on subways aren't the type to be very helpful to the police, and this crowd was no different. They were insulting and harassing the cop, trying to prevent the arrest. They didn't notice me arrive so, with the element of surprise on my side, I burst through the crowd and took hold of the prisoner before they could stop me. This made them really mad and they turned on me. I heard someone shout, 'Throw the cop on to the tracks.' Arms grabbed me and pushed me towards the edge of the platform. I had to let go of the prisoner as I struggled to resist, but there were too many of them and I could feel myself getting closer and closer to the train tracks. Coming from inside the tunnel I could see two enormous yellow headlights bearing down the tracks, and I could hear the roar of the train getting louder as it got closer. Just as I was on the edge of the platform, about to be pushed on to the tracks, I cried out, 'Jesus, help me!'

Suddenly two big black guys appeared out of the crowd, pushing people aside. 'Officer, follow us,' one of them said. 'Sure, I'll follow you anywhere,' I said, gratefully. Because the crowd was caught by surprise, I was able to get hold of the prisoner again before we made our way up out of the subway. The two black guys went in front, clearing the way, and the injured cop came behind me, his hand on my shoulder. Up on the street I pushed the prisoner into the back of the waiting patrol car and turned round to thank the guys who had saved us, but there were crowds of people milling around and I couldn't see them anywhere. I didn't want to hang around so I shouted out, 'Thanks for your help, guys,' and climbed into the back seat next to the prisoner. 'C'mon, let's go,' I said.

The wounded cop was sitting up front next to the driver, and as we left the scene he turned around to me and said, 'Mike, that was some job you did getting the prisoner through the crowd.'

'Yeah, I thought we were done for,' I said. 'Thank God for those two guys going ahead of us pushing people aside.'

'What two guys?'

'The two black guys who were pushing the crowds out of the way.'

'I didn't see no black guys helping us.'

'You must have seen them. They were talking to us, told us to follow them.'

'I didn't hear nothing.'

I was puzzled. I'd definitely seen and heard these two guys who had saved us. If it hadn't been for them, I figured I'd have been dead by now. But why hadn't the other cop seen them? Just then some words from the Bible came into my head: 'Are not all angels ministering spirits sent to serve those who will inherit salvation?' (Hebrews 1:14).

'Naah,' I thought, 'it can't have been.'

But I couldn't get the possibility out of my mind. I was a believer and I had certainly needed help. I stored the memory in my head and in my heart, but I didn't tell many people about it. It's not a smart thing to do, telling New York people that you're a cop who sees angels!

There was a new guy in the precinct. He was a Vietnam veteran, an established cop with a chestful of medals. In his time he'd seen soldiers and policemen crack under pressure, but he'd withstood it all – he had nothing to prove. His name was Billy, but we called him Batman. One day I was out on foot patrol when he spotted me.

'Hey, Mike, come over here.'

'Yeah, what's happening?'

'I'm gonna make an arrest. See that guy over there?'

He nodded his head and I followed his gaze.

'Yeah.'

'Well, he knows I'm after him, and every time he sees me he runs.'

'Okay, so?'

'You go stand over there. I'll count to ten and then I'll go up to him, and then when he runs, he'll be running right at you and you can stop him.'

I thought about that for a minute. The suspect didn't look too big.

'Okay, give me a minute to get over there.'

'Okay, we'll both count to ten.'

I walked across the street, counting to ten, and then I turned round. The suspect was charging like a locomotive straight towards me, and he was a lot bigger and stronger as he got closer. He suddenly saw that I was a cop and swerved to avoid me. I side-stepped him and he cannonballed into me, sending both of us right over the barricade and into an open hole, five feet deep, that had been dug by the Edison Electric Company.

'Waaaaaaaah!'

As I started to fall backwards, all I could think was: not only am I falling into this pit, but this huge guy is going to land on me.

Thud! We landed on the muddy earth at the bottom of the hole. I shook my head, looked around, and I couldn't believe it – I was on top of the other guy. It didn't make sense, he'd fallen in on top of me and the hole wasn't big or deep enough for us to have twisted round. But I didn't have time to worry about how it had happened; my immediate concern was how we were going to get out.

'Hey, Mike, you okay?'

I looked up and Batman was peering down at me.

'Yeah, I think so. Just get me outta here!'

Batman had already radioed for help and I could hear the familiar *whee, whee* of a police car as I spoke. We were soon both out of the pit.

'Thanks, Mike, you did a great job,' Batman winked at me.

I acknowledged his thanks but I felt as if I'd had a beating. I was aching all over, and my uniform was covered in mud. I followed Batman and his prisoner to the car and had just opened the door to get in when I noticed two black guys standing to one side, watching me. They looked vaguely familiar. They smiled and I nodded back, then I climbed in the car and closed the door. As we made our way back to the precinct, I relaxed, and thought some more about what had happened, how by rights I should have been the one to be at the bottom of the pit with the big guy on top of me – and then I realised where I'd last seen those two big black guys. Down the subway station.

Another night I made an arrest which meant I had to go to court to give evidence against the prisoner. It was a suffocating hot day and the train I was travelling on was full of people: commuters and shoppers going about their everyday business, and tourists, studying their maps, discussing their plans, how they were going to spend the day, what sights they were going to see. Because the train was so crowded I had to stand, and as I rocked to and fro with the motion of the train I listened to the talking and tried to place where the speakers came from. There were a couple of Japanese, and I thought I'd picked out an English accent, when suddenly I heard a low New York voice speaking into my ear, 'This is the day you die, pig.' I felt my assailant's hot breath on my skin and the cold of the gun barrel against my head. I froze helplessly as he pulled back the trigger. Then, out of the corner of my eye, I saw a black hand grabbing the barrel of the gun. I didn't need to be told what to do then; my reaction was instinctive. I turned on my attacker, disarmed him and bent his arm up behind his back. We were just pulling into a station, and as soon as the doors opened I pushed him out ahead of me on to the platform. The whole incident lasted two minutes at most. My main concern, once I had overpowered him, was to handcuff my prisoner and prevent him causing harm to me or any of the other passengers. In the confusion and panic that followed the incident I lost sight of the man who had saved me, but I had no doubt that it was my angel again.

I wasn't living a normal life – every day I could be facing life-threatening incidents such as these – and God had made a promise to watch over me. I depended on him every second of every tour of duty. Other cops in the district saw the miracles that happened in my life and they drew strength from God in me; they'd often ask me to put in a word for them with 'The Man Upstairs'.

In spite of this – all the deep joy I knew because of Jesus and the special protection I trusted God for, as well as my lovely Annie and growing family – there were many times when depression surfaced. I was on patrol one night in the subways when a guy tried to end his life by jumping in front of a train. He didn't die right away, but he lost a leg. In that subway, in the middle of the night, in the pitch dark, because the power had been switched off, I had to take a flashlight and crawl along the track, feeling my way, trying to find his missing limb. Finally my hand came into contact with this piece of human flesh, still warm and sticky, and the medics had to carry it back to the station where other medics were working on the guy. They took him and his leg off to hospital and I was left on the platform. I wandered out into the street – I needed some air – and as I walked, feeling completely alone, I asked God, 'Where are you tonight, Lord? You seem so distant.'

I was in what seemed like a never-ending battle. Every night I'd hear the same sounds: police sirens, gunshots, screaming, abuse. A night could seem like a year, and I wondered if I was ever going to get out of this job. I knew that God wanted me in the police force but that didn't stop me asking him, 'How much longer, Lord? How much more of this can I take?'

Part of the reason for me being in the police force was to help others. I saw many people in need and I tried the best I could to help them. When we know Jesus we have the power of God working through us, and if we are prepared to listen to the Holy Spirit and his guiding and let God lead us, then we can really help people.

One night I answered a call to a robbery. Arriving on the scene I was naturally anxious, full of fear, apprehensive as to what I would find, but ready to do whatever I had to. Most every night would be the same, the darkness bringing out the evil in people. This time one man had been shot dead and another man was lying, bleeding, on the floor. Two men had been arrested and the situation was under control when I arrived. I did what I could to help the man on the floor until the ambulance arrived, and then I stood back, preparing to return to my car. Suddenly someone grabbed my hand. It was Batman. His whole body was shaking and the tears were running down his cheeks. Now you have to remember that this guy was a good cop; he'd been through the conflict in Vietnam and he had medals for bravery; he wasn't a coward; yet here he was sobbing on the street.

'I'm gonna quit, Mike.'

I took him by the shoulders and led him back to the car.

'Get in, Billy,' I said, 'you can tell me about it.'

We sat together in the car and Batman talked, told me how he couldn't take it any more, all the death and violence and misery. I listened and at last, when he'd let it all out, I began, 'You know what, Billy, I remember when I felt like that.' And I started to share with Batman some of my past.

'You? You, Mike, you went through all this? But you're not like this now.'

'That's because I found someone who made a difference to my life.'

I went on to tell him about Jesus and the hope he gave me, and at 2.30 a.m., on the streets of Times Square, my good friend Batman was saved. We said the sinner's prayer together and Batman's life was changed. He became a regular cop for Christ.

A few of us used to meet up for coffee in one of our breaks each week and have a Bible study. Batman joined in and began to learn and understand things more. He was very enthusiastic and couldn't wait for our weekly sessions. I bumped into him on the stairs one day.

'Hey, Mike, we gonna have a Bible study today?'

'Sure, Billy, see you later.'

His life and attitude had changed so much in a few weeks, he was a joy to be around. But life and crime went on in New York City just as it always had. It was a hot morning and my partner Jimmy and I were on patrol when a 10:13 came on the radio. That meant an officer needed assistance. A cop was in trouble and shots had been fired. We had to cross town to get to the scene and we didn't need to be told when we'd arrived there. It was the morning rush hour and people were running around in all directions, screaming and yelling. Some were hiding behind parked cars, others just wanted to get as far away as they could from the scene. Jimmy stopped the car, and we jumped out and ran to the side of a building that gave us some cover. I peered around the corner. There was a policeman lying on his back in the street. He was covered in blood. There was another man in civilian clothes sitting on the pavement near the cop. He was also bleeding heavily. I looked around carefully – there was no sign of anyone else with a gun.

'Okay, Jimmy, I'm going to see what we can do for these guys.'

Jimmy nodded. I darted out on to the street. No shots were fired at me. I figured that the wounded civilian was the assailant and he was in no condition to put up a fight. He had his arms wrapped round himself and each time he breathed blood oozed out of his wounds. Another cop went through his pockets looking for a gun and found a police badge: he was a cop too.

'Okay, pal, the ambulance is on its way, you'll soon be all right,' I said, but I could see his eyes rolling and the colour draining from him. He was going into shock. The only thing I could think to do was to whisper in his ear, 'Jesus, Jesus, Jesus,' over and over again. Suddenly I thought I heard a shot go off. I spun round from the wounded man and crouched with my gun drawn in my hands outstretched in front of me. Then something happened to me. I could see people screaming but I couldn't hear them. I could see the flashing lights of the ambulance but I couldn't hear its siren. People were running all around me but I couldn't move. A policeman came up to me and said something but I couldn't hear what he said, I could only see his lips moving. Then a girl ran out of the crowd towards me. She grabbed my arm and said, 'Jesus loves you.' I snapped out of my state of shock, and then, for the first time, I turned around and looked at the cop dead on the floor.

'Oh, no.'

It was Batman. I fell to my knees and put my arms around him. I held him against me and looked up at the heavens. It was devastating, the saddest experience I had ever had at that point in my life. My brother in the Lord, Billy the Batman, dead from a gunshot wound. I had a tremendous feeling of loss inside me. It was a beautiful morning but I felt as empty as the clear blue sky up above me. Then I felt the Holy Spirit say, 'This day he's with me in paradise. Thank you for witnessing to my child.'

After the ambulance came, when Batman and the wounded cop were taken away and the area had been cleaned up, I stayed there for about an hour, just standing and thinking along with other cops who'd been on the scene. I had no real thoughts in my head. I'd only known Batman about three months, but I'd known him well enough to know he was a good cop and a good guy, the type you could easily get along with and like. I was going to miss him.

I cried out to God, 'How am I going to last on this job? Are my kids going to be fatherless? Lord, please take me out of here.' But there was no answer from God.

I finished work early that day and went home. I had gone into a traumatic state at the scene of the incident, and I suffered from a recurring nightmare. I had it again the night after Batman died. In it, water was coming over the side of a mountain and I was standing under it. The water was cool and refreshing at first, but then it changed to blood. I'd wake up screaming and Ann would have to grab my hand and pray over me until the anxiety had subsided. Every night for five nights after Batman's death I had this nightmare, and I became afraid to go to sleep. The following night I sat up in a chair, reading my Bible, trying, unsuccessfully, to stay awake. I had the dream again, but this time the water didn't turn to blood but stayed clear and pure. I knew then that I was healed, and I never had that nightmare again.

Because of what I'd been through I could have received a pension from the force on the grounds of depression. I'd been on the job about twelve years now, and I would have had a good pension – three-quarters of my salary tax-free for the rest of my life. In fact, if I'd taken it then my pension would have been considerably larger than my final pension! It was a tough decision. I asked the Lord, 'What do I do? Do I stay or do I go?' I really hoped he'd say, 'Go,' but he didn't.

As well as dealing with the pain of Batman's death, I had to accept that I was going to have to face much more of the same for as many years as God wanted me to stay in the police force. I really needed 'steadfast faith when all hell is coming against you'.

Chapter 14

With something like 700 miles of track running under the city and hundreds of stations, the easiest and quickest way to get round New York is on the subway. Native New Yorkers learn how to make sense of the maps with all the stations and routes crossing each other, but for strangers catching the subway for the first time it can be confusing. One of the things I enjoyed in my early days as a cop was being on a station and being approached by visitors to the city, who knew where they wanted to go but had no idea how to get there. It was great to meet so many different people and be able to help them, in a small way, to enjoy their visit.

To travel any distance across the city usually involves changing trains. For the journey I was making across town on this particular day I needed to change trains at 42nd Street. The train I was on pulled into the station, the doors opened, people piled out, and I should have gone with them but I couldn't move. Or really, my legs *wouldn't* move. I needed to get off the train to catch another one but, try as I might, I couldn't get one leg in front of the other. I stayed exactly where I was. The doors closed, the train started again and I was still on it. As soon as we'd pulled out of the station, my legs seemed to come back to life and I could move again. I had no idea what had happened to me. I thought maybe it was tiredness. I probably just needed a break. I wondered if I should go see the doctor, see if he thought I needed some sick leave. I wasn't worried now about going off sick, I had passed my probationary period and I was well respected as a cop. But right then I needed to get back to the 42nd Street station to catch my connection. It wasn't a big problem – I could get off at the next stop, change platforms, and catch another train back a stop – but it made my journey longer and was an inconvenience I could have done without.

When the train pulled into the next stop and the doors opened, my legs worked fine and I stepped on to the platform with no difficulty. I had no pain, no numbness, nothing to suggest anything unusual had happened. I started to make my way out of the subway ready to cross the street to get back to the right station. As I walked up the steps, I saw two cops ahead of me, standing talking. I heard one of them say, 'I'm gonna blow my brains out.' The other one said something, shrugged his shoulders and walked off. Whether he didn't believe that his friend would kill himself or whether he knew that he would and felt helpless to stop him and didn't want to watch, he didn't hang around.

It's not unusual for cops to kill themselves. The pressure and the depression that come with the job can wear down even the toughest. It's hard for a policeman to admit that he has a problem; he has a macho image he feels he has to live up to, saying to himself, 'I'm a cop, how can I have a problem?' I knew the situation only too well; I'd been there myself. Now I knew why I hadn't been able to move my legs and get off at the right station – God wanted me here for this reason. I walked over to the cop. He was standing alone, his shoulders hunched, his head down and his face haggard.

'Hi, how you doing?' I asked.

'Who are you?'

'I'm Mike. I heard what you said to the other guy.'

'Well, it ain't none of your business.'

'It becomes my business when I see a fellow cop in trouble, when I see a fellow man who wants to kill himself.'

'Well, you can unmake it your business.'

'Fine,' I said, 'I thought maybe if you'd listen to me for a few minutes I might be able to help you, give you a little hope, but if you're not interested, just do me a favour – give me a few minutes to get out of here before you do this. I don't want to be a witness.'

I turned and began to walk away, praying as I did, 'Jesus, give me the right words. How can I help this guy?'

'Hey!'

I turned around.

'You calling me?'

'Yeah, I'm calling you, come here.'

'What's up?'

'You just said you were going to help me, you were going to talk to me. You can't walk away now. What ya got to say?'

'Okay, let me talk to you for a little while, ask you a few questions. I'm not a psychiatrist, I'm just a cop, but I've had my problems too. I've had times when I would have welcomed dying, but you know what? I found there's an answer. It became my hope and I know it's the hope that's helped other cops.'

'Yeah, well, what is it?'

'Tell me first what's going on in your life right now to cause you to want to take your own life.'

'It ain't none of your business.'

'Then I can't help you.'

All the time this was going on, I was asking the Holy Spirit for help to be able to see clearly what was the root of his problems and to find the right way to be able to help him.

'Okay, okay. I put $3,000 down on a house I'm having built. Two days ago, my wife and I signed the contract. Today she left me with my kids. She said, "I can't take this any more," and she turned round and walked out. I don't want that house, I want to die and I'm going to kill myself.'

'Hey, man, just listen to me a minute. Maybe there is hope.'

I didn't want to tell him that his wife would come back and everything would be all right – I didn't know if she would and I didn't want to raise his expectations only for them to collapse again later. We talked some more and at last I said, 'Here's the answer I found. Do you want to hear it?'

'Yeah.'

'There is a hope and it's in a person, and this person loves you very much.'

'What you talking about? Who loves me? My wife doesn't.'

'Just let me finish,' I said, and I started to tell him about Jesus.

'Whoa, whoa, no, man, I don't want none of that Jesus stuff.'

'Fine,' I said, 'then I can't help you no more. I gave you the answer and I can't do no more than that.'

I turned around and started walking away, praying, 'Lord, Lord.'

'Hey you, come over here.'

I looked round.

'You talking to me?'

'Yeah, come back over here.'

'You sure this time?'

'Yeah, now, you say this Jesus can help me? How?'

'Did you have some Bible teaching when you were a kid? Do you believe in Jesus, that he existed?'

'Yeah, I guess.'

'Well, the Bible tells us that Jesus not only died for our sins and our hurts but he rose from the dead and he's in heaven. If that's true, then he's alive and he can help you.'

'But how do you know that's true?'

'That's when you gotta have faith. I've got that faith because I've seen Jesus at work in my life and in the lives of others, and that helps me to know it's true. If you've got the faith to turn to Jesus, then he will help you. Will you let me pray with you? Pray for a miracle, maybe that you and your wife will get back together?'

'Where we gonna pray?'

I looked around. I knew he didn't want to pray in the street.

'There's a store over there, let's go in there.'

We walked into the store. I called the storekeeper over.

'You got a back room?'

'Yeah, why?'

'This guy's not feeling too good. Could we go in and sit down for a few minutes?'

'Yeah, sure. You want me to call an ambulance?'

'No, that's okay, he'll be all right when he's rested.'

The storekeeper nodded and pointed to a door at the side of the shop and we made our way in. There were a few chairs and a table in there. We sat down opposite each other.

'Do you want to pray to ask Jesus to come into your heart?'

He hesitated for a moment. I prayed silently, then he said, 'Yeah, okay.'

'Hold my hands then and we'll pray.'

'Whaaat? Hold your hands?'

'Yeah.'

'But what if someone comes in and sees us sitting here holding hands?'

'An hour and a half ago you wanted to shoot yourself out on the street with thousands of people walking by. You didn't mind them seeing your brains all over the sidewalk, now you worry about people seeing us holding hands!'

'Well, put a chair against the door first, just in case.'

So in that little back room we held hands and prayed, and he accepted Christ into his life.

Soon after that, he and his wife got back together, and a few months later Ann and I were invited to a house-warming party in their newly completed house. He went on to make sergeant in the police force, and he is still part of Cops for Christ and being used by God today.

It wasn't Bible-bashing that saved him. Because I let the Holy Spirit lead me, God, working through me, saved him.

Tourists who come to New York are fascinated by the cops. They've seen us on the TV and in movies, and they've read about us. I'd be on patrol and I'd often hear people, especially kids, saying, 'Look, it's a New York City policeman.' I must have had my picture taken with tourists hundreds of times. I'd be standing on a corner and they'd come up and say, 'Hi, do you mind if I have my photo taken with you?' I'd always say, 'Yeah, go ahead but, hey, send me a copy.' One French guy did, too. I still have it somewhere.

If I saw kids with their parents, I'd wave and maybe go over and chat with them. Sometimes they'd ask me to tell them a bit about life as a cop in New York. I'd start off with some police stories and then, because I never liked to miss an opportunity, I'd tell them about the difference Jesus made in my life. I can't remember how many people accepted Jesus as their saviour after I'd witnessed to them while we were talking. It was also good public relations for the department to have a good rapport with the people.

So my ministry grew, on the subways, in the streets and in prisons.

In prisons, I really had a captive audience. They kept six to eight men together in holding pens, and when I had to take someone in I'd stop and talk to them all. I'd say, 'Hey, you guys, listen up,' and I'd share the gospel with them. Many people were saved in that way. If they asked Jesus into their lives, I would take their names and write them down in my pocketbook.

There were times I was able to meet them and try to get some sort of help for them, whether that was somewhere to live or a job or help to fight an addiction. Sometimes I'd find them a place with Teen Challenge, an organisation that would house and support them as they rebuilt their lives. Whatever was needed, I made sure to get them help.

In the mid 1980s New York was gripped by party fever. I don't recall exactly what the celebrations were for, but there were parties everywhere. One of the biggest celebrations was happening in the southern tip of Manhattan. Manhattan is on an island, linked by bridges, ferries and tunnels to the other New York boroughs of Brooklyn, Queens, Staten Island and the Bronx; the island gets narrower towards the southern tip. The organisers of the celebrations were expecting around three million people to show up for the event, and I think every cop in New York City was ordered into work for four straight days.

I had been on the force for a while now and I'd earned some respect from my fellow officers, who knew I could be relied on to treat them right. At the start of this celebration, I reported for roll call as usual.

'How ya doing, Willy?' I said to the sergeant on the desk that night.

He had his head bowed over some papers and he didn't look up or say anything.

I said again, 'Willy, how are ya?'

He still didn't look up. I figured it must be something important he was reading and I didn't want to disturb him too much, so I said, 'Willy, do ya mind if I look at roll call to see what my assignment is?'

At last he looked at me and sighed, 'Mike, I'm sorry I have to do this to you.'

From his face I could see it must be something bad; he could hardly bear to look in my eyes. He must have been dreading me reporting for duty.

'What's the matter, Willy? What's my assignment?'

'I have to give you the worst area of the lot tonight.'

It was one of the unwritten laws that the more experienced officers, the ones who were almost considered veterans, didn't get the worst assignments. They had worked for years to earn some kind of privileges.

'So why'd ya give me the worst area, Willy?'

'Because you're with a rookie.'

The police force was on such a high state of alert that every officer, however inexperienced, was needed to be part of the police presence on the streets; and it was another unwritten law that, under such conditions, a rookie shouldn't go out alone. I understood the situation and I sighed, 'It's okay, Willy. Who is he?'

The sergeant pointed across the room at a young Chinese officer.

'That's him, Officer Chung.'

I went over and introduced myself, then said, 'Come on, then, Chung, let's get going.'

As we were going down the stairs, Chung said, 'You no mind if I drive?'

'It'd be my pleasure,' I said. I had no great desire to drive the car through the crowds that night and he considered it an honour to drive, so it suited us both. We made our way across the car park to where the patrol car was waiting for us. I opened the passenger door and got in. Officer Chung opened the trunk (boot). I looked over my shoulder out of the back window at the raised trunk. I didn't know what he was doing but I figured he was putting something in there. At last he shut it, but then he came round the side, opened the back door and peered in. He checked under the seats and down the back of the seats. I wondered if he'd lost something, but I didn't see how he could have done as he hadn't been in this car before. Finally he opened the driver's door, and got in. 'At last,' I thought, 'maybe we can go now.' But he wasn't ready yet. He leaned across me and opened the glove compartment. That was it, I'd had enough.

'What are you doing?' I yelled.

He looked at me in surprise.

'I look for dead bodies.'

'Whaaat?'

'They tell us in police academy, get in car, check for dead bodies or bad things, you don't want get in trouble for something you haven't done.'

'Chung,' I said, 'just shut up and drive the car, will ya?'

As he switched on the engine I explained some things to him. I knew he'd read every comic book, seen every film in which there's a cop chase. I knew he was anxious and he wanted to get in there with the action, but I also knew we had to take it easy. With all the potholes in the roads and the people on the streets, it wasn't safe to drive fast.

'This whole area is very intense,' I said. 'There will be thousands of people everywhere on the streets. Remember we're on patrol and don't go any faster than fifteen miles an hour. And another thing: don't put the siren on. We'll know if there's trouble and we'll go, but we don't want to cause a panic and end up with a riot on our hands, so whatever happens, do not put on the siren. You got that?'

'Sure, I got that, no faster than fifteen miles an hour and no siren.'

'Okay, let's go.'

As he drove, I talked to Chung, asked him questions about his family and what made him become a cop. He wasn't long out of the police academy, and talking to him brought back my own memories, some of which I'd rather have forgotten. I know I wouldn't have survived if it hadn't been for Jesus. I asked Chung what religion he was.

'I'm a Buddhist. What are you?'

'I'm a Christian, I believe in Jesus.'

'Oh yes, Jesus, good. I heard of Jesus.'

'Do you know much about being a Buddhist?'

Chung shrugged his shoulders, 'No, not much.'

'Do you mind if I tell you a bit about Jesus, then?' I asked him.

'Sure, that's okay.'

I believe that part of the job that the Lord wanted me to do was to witness to young cops, so I started telling Chung about Jesus and the gospel. I didn't want to cram too much information into him, but there were some important things I thought he needed to hear. It was up to him what he did with them then.

As it happened, I didn't have time to tell him too much because a 10:13 came over the radio. That meant a patrolman was in trouble and needed assistance.

'Okay, Chung, let's . . .'

I was going to say 'take it easy and make our way over there' but I didn't have the chance. Before the words were out of the radio operator's mouth, Chung had his foot down on the accelerator. I watched helplessly as the speedometer needle went up – fifteen, twenty, twenty-five – and then *whee*, *whee*, *whee*, the siren was going as well.

'Chung, no!' I yelled.

But it was no good, Chung was in another world, the world of *French Connection*, of movie stars and car chases. He was staring straight ahead, his hands tightly gripping the wheel. This was the greatest moment in his life. I kept yelling at him but I couldn't get his attention. I was mad at him but I understood what was motivating him. I remembered the early excitement of being a cop, when I thought I was going to save the world, stop every wrongdoer in New York, when I still thought that I could make a difference.

But right then we were approaching a busy intersection controlled by traffic lights and the lights were red against us. Traffic laws are the same for everyone, even cops with their siren on. We don't have a special right of way. If the light's red, you're supposed to stop. Chung showed no sign of slowing down – if anything he was going faster. I was still yelling at him and he was still Popeye Doyle. I could see a yellow cab approaching the intersection, coming from the street to our right. The lights were still against us, and the driver of the yellow cab, oblivious to the police car hurtling towards him from the side, saw green lights and kept going. We were headed straight for him; there was no way we could miss. I closed my eyes, and curled over as best I could, bracing myself for the impact. 'What a way to die,' I thought. 'All that I've been through, the shootings and stabbings I've seen, and I'm gonna die in a collision with a rookie at the wheel.'

I waited for the impact.

It didn't come. After a few seconds I opened my eyes, lifted my head and looked around. We were on the other side of the intersection. We'd somehow missed the yellow cab. I looked over my shoulder and could see it disappearing off up the street to the left.

'Chung,' I said, 'what happened? How come we didn't hit that car? We were heading right for it, we should have hit it. What happened?'

Chung was looking straight ahead, his eyes wide, his face drained of colour.

'Chung, what happened?'

'We go through car. We go through car. We go through car.'

He kept repeating those four words, as if he couldn't believe he was saying it. And it was hard to believe. I don't know what happened. I didn't see anything because I had my eyes closed, but I know that we had been on a sure collision course and it was a miracle that we were still alive.

'Chung,' I said, 'I don't know whether we went through that car or over it, but I do know that Jesus saved our lives tonight.'

'Jesus saved our lives tonight,' Chung repeated the words thoughtfully.

He took the rest of the journey a little slower, and when we arrived at the call there were already a lot of cops there. Chung leapt out of the car and ran over to a group of them, saying, 'We go through car, Jesus save our lives tonight, we go through car,' over and over again. A couple of the guys stopped and listened to him. They looked at each other, puzzled, and then one of them looked over at our car and saw me and it all became clear to him.

'Aw, he's with Mikey.'

The other cop rolled his eyes, 'Ah, Mikey, right, so that's why Jesus saved his life, yeah.'

They were guys from my precinct, guys I knew well. They weren't being nasty, they just understood what Chung was saying now. One of them got out his pen and memobook.

'Okay, now, Officer, for report purposes, where was Jesus at the time he saved you? Was he on the hood (bonnet)? Or on the roof? Or was he travelling in the trunk? We'll need to write all this in the report.'

Chung looked confused but thoughtful.

'Not in trunk,' he said. 'I check in trunk before.'

'Come on, Chung,' I said, 'don't listen to them. We know what happened tonight even if no one else believes us.'

I never saw Chung again after that assignment. He worked in a different area usually – he'd only been brought in for the policing of the celebrations – but I often wondered whatever happened to him. Maybe he ended up becoming an evangelist for China . . . now there's a thought.

Chapter 15

It was 2.00 a.m. on a warm and quiet night in summer and I was on duty in the patrol car. My tour of duty had been unusually uneventful so far, and I was grabbing the opportunity to sit back and relax for a moment. As I sat there, a wave of overwhelming oppression swept over me, shattering the calm. This was different from the depression I still suffered, brought on by the fear and anxiety initiated by my job. This was an awareness of the presence of evil around me. It wasn't uncommon for me to feel oppression, but this night it was very intense, like a physical weight on my shoulders.

I got out of the car and began to pray. I walked round and round the car, praying as the Holy Spirit led me, until at last I felt a deep peace come over me and I felt strengthened and ready to face whatever evil was lurking round the corner. I knew something real bad was going to happen, that there was going to be big trouble on the streets of New York this night. I continued on patrol, my alertness peaked now, wondering and waiting for what was going to happen.

At about a quarter to five, I went back to the district for a break. Jimmy was there. He and I had known each other now for years, often working as partners – in fact I'd worked with

Jimmy more than any other officer – and we were real close. I stopped to have a cup of coffee with him and I could see from his face that there was something he wanted to tell me.

'Guess what, Mike?' he said.

'What's that, Jimmy?'

'I've put my papers in. I've only got thirty-four more days till I retire.'

'No kidding?'

'Naah, thirty-four more days and then I'll be out of this job for good.'

'Hey, Jimmy, that's great news,' I said. 'I'm really happy for you.'

We carried on talking for a while, Jimmy full of his plans for his retirement, what he was going to do when he didn't have to patrol the streets and subways of New York any more, how he was going to be able to spend some more time with his family, how he was so looking forward to doing all the things he wanted to do. We remembered stuff we'd been through, like him getting saved in a sewer!

'You know how I used to hate this job, Mike? I don't hate it any more, but I'll sure be glad to be out of it.'

He stood up then.

'I'd better get back on patrol, do the job while I'm still here.'

'Okay, Jimmy,' I said, 'but, hey, only thirty-four more tours to do!'

I stood up and Jimmy kissed me on the cheek and said, ' I love you, Mike,' and then he left. I stayed for a while, just sitting and thinking. I was happy for Jimmy but I had very mixed emotions. I was going to miss him. We'd been through such a lot; we'd shared good times and bad. We'd been in life-threatening situations together. There were periods when I probably saw more of him than I did of Ann!

And there were other less happy thoughts that ran through my head at the same time: I've got years left to go; how am I gonna last? do I have the strength to keep going?

My train of thought was interrupted by a message coming over my radio: a 10:13, an officer in need of assistance. The location given wasn't far from the district and I ran out to see what I could do to help. The incident had taken place in a popular shopping area. There was a staircase leading from the subway to the street level. As I arrived, a man was running down the stairs, screaming horrifically.

When he reached the mezzanine area I stopped him, grabbed him by the shoulders, and said, 'What's the matter? What's happened?' He could hardly speak he was so scared.

'Up the stairs,' he pointed, 'up the stairs.'

'Yeah, yeah,' I said, 'what's up the stairs?'

'A cop, a cop's just been shot.'

'Oh, no,' I sighed. I released my hold on him. Now I knew what the Holy Spirit had been preparing me for earlier – the shooting of a cop. Any kind of violence was difficult to deal with, but the shooting of a fellow officer was worse. That made it very personal. I was still the only policeman on the scene, to my knowledge, and I had to go up and investigate. I couldn't see what was at the top of the stairs – it was possible there was an armed maniac waiting there to shoot any cop who got close, and I had to be prepared for that. I drew out my gun and made my way slowly up the stairs, my gun in my outstretched arms ahead of me, ready to shoot. I was real scared. It was only the grace of God and the courage and confidence he gave me that enabled me to get up those stairs. Without him my legs wouldn't have moved. When I was far enough up the stairs, I stuck my head up and glanced around, then ducked back down quickly. No shots were fired. I walked up another step and stuck my head up again. The sun was just rising and it was light enough for me to see right into the street. Everything seemed quiet. I looked to the left: there was nobody there. I looked straight ahead: that was clear too. I looked to the right: there was a police officer lying on the floor surrounded by blood. It was Jimmy. I climbed the remaining steps and ran over to him. He was perfectly still and I knew he was dead.

'Oh no, Lord, don't let him die,' I cried, 'Lord, you can raise him, it's not too late, don't let him die, Lord.'

Some more cops who had responded to the call arrived soon and took Jimmy's body to hospital. I was stunned and saddened at the loss of my friend, but I was still a policeman and I had a job to do. One of my duties was to block off the scene of the crime; another was to go and help catch his killer.

There were witnesses who'd seen what had happened. It turned out that Jimmy had been ejecting a homeless person from the subway when the guy had turned on him, taken Jimmy's own gun out of his holster and shot him with it. It took us a while to find the homeless man. He was high on drugs, out of his mind, without any real knowledge of what he'd done, and he still had Jimmy's gun on him. When the homeless man was brought into the district a few hours later, I hated him. I was angry and my heart was full of hatred for the man who'd killed my partner. 'Why, Lord,' I asked, 'why did he have to do it? Why did you let him kill Jimmy? And don't tell me to forgive him now.'

I wanted answers from God and I suppose I wanted to believe that God hated the man the same as I did, but the Holy Spirit just said, 'I love you and I love him too.'

There were certain matters that had to be gone through and I had to do them. I had to officially escort the man and then protect him, ensure his safety while he was in custody. His hair was long and unkempt and his clothes were torn and dirty, but when I looked closely at him, beneath all that, I could see that he was very scared. It was the evil effect that the drugs had had on him that caused him to become a killer. It wasn't an excuse, but I could begin to see something of what God wanted me to do. I knew I had to witness to him. It was the last thing I wanted to do at that moment and I had to force myself to do it, but I knew it was right.

And later, when I got home and the awfulness of the situation struck me again, I said, 'Lord, I can't take any more of this killing and violence and evil. There must be other work I could do for you. Will you please take me out of all this?'

But God stayed quiet.

Coping with Jimmy's death was one of the most difficult things I ever had to do. The days and weeks following were the hardest time of my life, and it was only God's grace that got me through it. I still think of Jimmy today, all these years later: sometimes I laugh, maybe when I think about him being saved in a sewer, and other times I cry.

Jimmy thought he had thirty-four more days to go until he retired, but he only had a few hours before he died. Many of us live our lives as if we have for ever, but in reality today could be our final day. I felt the Holy Spirit say to me, 'Tell the people all we have is today. Husbands, love your wives. Be at peace with all men.' Jimmy's death truly showed me that all we have is today.

At roll call the sergeant was solemn and I knew there was something up. He gave us our assignments for the night and then said, 'Before you go there's something I have to say. We would value your prayers for a retired police officer who is very sick. The doctors say he only has two days to live. He used to work out of this precinct – some of you may remember him. His name is Shamus Dillon.'

Oh no, I thought, not Scotty.

Scotty and I went way back. We'd come out of police academy together, we'd started out in the transit division in the same precinct, and we'd been on roll call together the night he'd been seriously injured. The knife attack had had a devastating effect on him, damaging him both physically and mentally, and he'd taken early retirement on health grounds. I hadn't seen him for a number of years but I was shocked by the news. I went up to the desk sergeant.

'Hey, Sarge, any chance I could change my tour?'

'Why, Mikey, what's up?'

'I knew that police officer real well – we graduated from police academy together – and I just don't feel like working tonight.'

'Sure, Mike, ya got it.'

I went home and told Ann. She sat with me and we spent some time praying together for Scotty and his family. He'd moved after he'd retired and he and his wife now lived upstate, about two hours' journey from us.

'I'd like to go and see Scotty tomorrow, Ann,' I said.

Without hesitating, Ann replied, 'I'll come with you.'

The next morning we bundled up our son Michael, who was a toddler then, and I gathered together a Bible, a tract and some oil. The only oil I could find in the house was the stuff Ann used to cook with, but I figured it would do. I wanted to pray over Scotty – I didn't know if he'd let me but I wanted to be prepared. We drove across the city and upstate to the address we had.

When we got there, Scotty's daughter opened the door and showed us into the room where her mom was sitting on the couch.

'Hi, Jane,' I said, 'remember us?'

'Mike, Ann, come on in,' Jane got up and hugged us both. 'It's good of you to come,' she said, and then she started crying. 'He's in pretty bad shape, you know, Mike.'

'I know, Jane,' I said, 'they told us at roll call. Is it okay if I go up and see him, maybe pray with him?'

'I don't know if he'll even know you're there.'

'That's okay, I can still pray for him.'

I went up the stairs leaving Ann with Jane. As I climbed the stairs I asked God for the right things to pray for Scotty. I walked into his room. Even though I knew things were bad I was shocked at the sight of him lying in the bed, his eyes closed. I walked over to his bedside and knelt down beside him. I put my mouth close to his ear and said, 'Scotty, it's me, Mike DiSanza. I don't know if you can hear me but I believe you can. I want to let you know that God loves you and that I love you, brother, and I'm going to pray for you. The Bible tells us to anoint the sick with oil, and that's what I'm going to do. I'm putting a little drop of oil on your forehead now and then I'm going to pray.'

After I'd finished, I stood up and looked at his face for a few minutes, then I went back downstairs to join the others. There were a number of other cops there, guys I'd worked with over the years, and we greeted each other. I talked some more to Jane and her daughter, and Ann helped making cups of coffee and sandwiches for the visitors who'd come to say goodbye to Scotty. Later on, when there was just Jane and Ann and me sitting round the kitchen table, Scotty walked in.

'Scotty?' Jane stared at her husband. He hadn't been out of bed for weeks. I jumped up and pulled out a chair, 'Here, sit here, Scotty.'

'Thanks, Mike,' he said, smiling the same beautiful Scottish smile he always had.

Jane was still stunned but I said, 'Praise the Lord. Jesus loves you, Scotty, and he wants you to come to him right now and pray for forgiveness.'

And right there and then, sitting at the kitchen table, Scotty gave his life to Jesus.

He went on to live for several years after that, and I thank the Lord for his miraculous power at work.

I was a veteran now. Seventy per cent of the guys I'd joined up with were either retired or dead, and at police functions, I couldn't help but realise that I was getting older. I was also aware how much the young new cops depended on me. I saw they had the same fears I'd had, still had, and I tried to help them to deal with their anxieties by explaining to them the difference Jesus had made in my life. Ann ran a support group for cops' wives, and many of the younger ones turned to her because she understood what it was like coping with long hours and the threat of death at any time.

One day the captain called me into his office. He looked pleased about something.

'Sit down, Mikey, I've got some news to tell you.'

He went on to say that the mayor of New York was concerned about the number of homeless people on the streets. The numbers ran into thousands, and there was to be a new initiative to deal with the problem. A special unit was to be set up that would cruise the streets each night, pick up the homeless and take them into night shelters.

'The thing is, Mike, the cops who man these units will have to be the right type of people. They will have to be veterans, used to dealing with people while not inciting violence. They'll also have to be tough, because there will probably be times when they come across wanted men who'll have to be arrested. And perhaps most of all, they will need compassion for their fellow man.'

'That sounds good, Captain. It's certainly time the city did something about the problem of homelessness.'

'Yeah, Mike, that's what I thought you'd say,' the captain beamed. 'Your name has been mentioned as someone who'd be right for the job. I'm so proud of you, Mike, one of my boys hand-picked for this special task. You know, the guys tell me, that Mikey Di, that's one guy they love to work with.'

I couldn't believe it. I had no idea that I was so highly thought of. I'd just done my best to do my job as well as I could. It's true that we don't know the effect our work has on people, but they do notice, and even in dark dingy depressing areas we can be a light and make a difference.

The first homeless unit to be set up worked Harlem and Times

Square. There were two vans, with two men and a driver on each. The city provided the overalls we had to wear – we came into contact with some less than clean individuals – and the vans. We wore our police badges on chains at all times and different coloured headbands round our hats. The headbands identified us to other cops as police officers. On the vans we carried sandwiches and soup to give to the homeless we picked up before taking them to one of the city shelters for the night. There they were de-loused if necessary and nurses were on hand to treat minor physical illnesses.

The city had gone through a financial crisis, and in an attempt to save money many hospital wards had been closed and people let out of mental institutions into the care of a community that, on the whole, didn't care. Many of the homeless men and women were mentally or emotionally damaged; others were in and out of prison. The van held about thirty people when it was full, and I'd look around and see all the sad young men and women, their faces older than their years. Whenever I had the opportunity, I'd take a stool and sit down with them and talk to them. The Holy Spirit gave me the discernment to understand their hurts. When I started talking, they'd stare at me with their blank eyes.

'Listen, guys and gals,' I'd say, 'I know you've had your troubles. I know what it's like to have troubles, I've been there, and I want to share some things with you that have helped me.'

They didn't understand at first. They were surprised that I even bothered to talk to them.

'I don't know how you got into this situation, but it doesn't really matter whether you ended up on the streets after being in jail or a mental hospital. I want to tell you that there is still hope.'

When I said that word 'hope' it always got their attention. It might only have been in a small way, a head looking up or eyes turned towards me, but it attracted them. People always want to know that there is hope, even in the deepest despair.

I'd go on and share a bit of my story, how Jesus gave me the hope to carry on, and then I'd ask, 'Does anyone here on this van want to know that hope? Do you want Jesus to come into your life and forgive any sin you've ever committed? Will you bow your heads now while I pray?'

I'd wait a minute and about 90 per cent of them would bow their heads; then I'd say, 'Put up your hand if you'd like Jesus to come into your life.'

Every night hands would go up into the air, and I really believe the commitment many of them made in the van. If they received Jesus in their spirit then they had eternal life. Many of the people we saw on the van would die within a year of us meeting them, either from illnesses brought on by living rough, or from drug-related incidents, or violence. Many of them had deep mental problems, but I believe that they understood salvation when I explained it, and that God saved many of them. Around three thousand people must have been brought to Jesus this way as God blessed me for doing what he wanted in this unit through the years. Although they were homeless, many physically or mentally impaired, each one had a special place in my heart.

Chapter 16

The homeless unit was regarded as a success and a second one was set up in Brooklyn. The unit I worked with had me continuing to work the streets of Harlem and Times Square at night, taking homeless individuals into the city shelters.

Among the people we were dealing with, many had suicidal tendencies, some were wanted by the law, and others were very sick. We often had to make arrests or take people to hospital, and we encountered violence on a nightly basis. I was involved in as many hand-to-hand situations as ever, and if anything I saw even more tragedy than on my previous patrol duties. It still caused me a lot of depression. Throughout my police career I had fought a constant battle with fear and anxiety, and even then – with eighteen years of service behind me and a God-given sense of security – there were times when I was weighed down.

One cold rainy night the van stopped at a red traffic light. I was up front in the van and I could see a young Spanish boy, maybe sixteen or seventeen years old, standing on a corner. It was the early hours of the morning and his clothes were torn and soaking wet. I shouted to him, 'Hey, you, get up on the van.'

He didn't move. The van was a familiar sight around the area; many people knew its route and waited to be picked up at the same spot each night. I figured maybe he was new to the area and he didn't know who we were.

'It's okay,' I said, 'we've got food and hot soup on here. We'll take you somewhere dry to spend the night. Come on, get in.'

He still didn't move and his face showed no emotion. The lights changed and the van driver said, 'What's he doing? Is he getting in or what?'

I looked at the boy again and this time I saw that his leg was deformed. It would be difficult for him to climb up the van steps. I said to the driver, 'Pull over there for a minute, will you? I'll have to get out and help him.'

The driver moved the van and parked at the side of the road. I got out and walked back to the boy.

'Do you want to get on the van?' I asked him.

He didn't reply, just stared at me. I figured that he hadn't said no, so I picked him up and carried him back on to the van. He wasn't difficult to carry: there was nothing to him. I gave him a sandwich, and I have never seen a boy eat anything so quick. Back at the shelter we found him some dry clothes and got him some medical treatment. He still wasn't talking, so I called him José for lack of anything better. He was just one of hundreds of homeless people in New York. Every night after that José would wait on the same corner for the van to pick him up. He never said anything and he showed no emotion whatsoever. His eyes were cold and sad.

I began to feel a real compassion for José. I felt sorry for him, but I liked him as well. He was a handsome boy, with his brown skin and big black eyes, and I just longed to see him smile.

Weeks passed. Sometimes we wouldn't see José for a few days and then he'd show up again, and I'd help him on the van and he'd have his sandwiches and soup. He kept himself at a distance from everyone. I wondered what had made him like that, if he'd been abused or if he'd become close to people only to have them let him down and hurt him. He didn't talk and I didn't try to make him. I was just glad to see him on the van, getting food and shelter.

I was still a policeman, doing a policeman's job, but I also had a ministry on the van and in the shelter. There would be about two thousand people put up for the night in the shelter; when we'd rounded some up and dropped them off, and after they'd eaten, I'd go into the dormitory with my Bible, sit down on a bed and start talking to them. People would gather round and listen to me. They came to know me and began to trust me, and when I walked in they'd grab my arm and say, 'Hi, Mike, you reading the Bible tonight?'

I'd look at some of them and think, 'My Lord, these guys are capable of turning round and killing a man in seconds,' and yet I had no fear. God had placed me there and he gave me a perfect peace about it. So I'd get out my Bible and say, 'Listen up, guys, I'm going to share the word of God with you.'

At that many of the people would gather round me. I never knew their names – most gave false names anyway, and I never met so many Joe Browns or Charlie Smiths! – but they all gathered round the bed as I shard Jesus with them. I'd tell them a little of my story or read from the Bible. I went out of my way to explain salvation to them because I knew it was the only thing that could touch them. I kept it simple.

'God loves you no matter what the world thinks, and Jesus came to die for every sin you ever committed.'

It had an effect. The love of God is real, and it has the power to touch people.

'Don't go on how you look or how you feel. It doesn't matter what others think about you. Just go in faith to God. I'm no better than you, I'm the least of the brethren, but I love you and Jesus loves you.'

Then I'd have an altar call, ask if anyone wanted to ask

Jesus into their life, give them the chance to act on what they'd heard.

One night in the van I shared the word of God and, as always, I asked if anyone wanted Jesus. It was a still night and there was silence in the van. Then José lifted his hand. He'd been coming on the van now for nearly a year; he must have heard the altar call hundreds of times. I was so thrilled I was clenching my fist in my hand, 'Oh, thank you, Jesus,' I cried.

Afterwards I went and sat next to José and we talked for about a quarter of an hour, sharing things from our lives. Then I asked him, 'José, what happened tonight? You've heard me ask many times before. What made you put up your hand tonight?'

His eyes were no longer blank but shining, and he said, 'I listened to you talking about Jesus. I didn't know Jesus and I didn't think he knew or cared about me, but I know that you love Jesus and you've shown that you care about me. I love you and I want to be with Jesus.'

I hugged José to me. 'I am so happy tonight, José,' I said. 'There's a prayer we can say: it's called the sinner's prayer. I'll say it first and I want you to listen to it carefully. If you agree with what I say, I want you to say "Amen" at the end. Do you understand? Is that all right?'

'Yes, Mike.'

Then I prayed the sinner's prayer with José. I really wanted him to say it but I wanted to be sure that he understood what he was saying. As soon as I got to the end, he said 'Amen' in a loud clear voice.

I looked at him, and for the first time in a year I saw a smile come on his face. I hugged him and yelled, 'Hallelujah!' I was so excited – I couldn't have been more excited if heaven itself had come down.

We saw a lot of sadness in the homeless unit. Many people died on the streets from tuberculosis or pneumonia as well as cancer or heart disease. Sometimes we'd get called out and we'd see faces we recognised, guys or gals who'd often been on the van with us. I was so grateful that many of them had come to know the Lord before they died, and I thank God for the opportunity he gave me to be a witness for him among the homeless. These were hurting people who were lost, and very few people cared about them. The average person in the street would just walk by them. I was so glad that the Lord gave me compassion and love for these people, and a commitment to them. I thank God that he chose me for this assignment before the earth ever began.

My partner on the van was Louie. I knew him by sight because we'd been in the same precinct, but I didn't know him well because we worked different areas and tours. Like me, he'd been in the police force about nineteen years, and before that he'd been in Vietnam. I knew he was street smart, a guy who wouldn't back out if it came to trouble: in other words, a good guy to have as a partner. We got along real well – we were both Italian and veterans – but as I came to know him a little better I discovered that he had hang-ups, like all of us. He didn't share his problems or his personal life with me, so all I could do was pray for him, and we got along just fine.

One night out with the homeless unit, there was some serious trouble and we had to make an arrest. It was near the end of our shift so we took the guy back to the precinct, got him finger-printed and stopped to do the paperwork. When we'd finished it was time to go home and we walked outside together.

'Okay, Mike, see ya tomorrow.'

I didn't reply and Louie turned to look at me.

'I said, "see ya tomorrow", Mike.'

I was still standing there, saying nothing.

'Are you okay, Mike? Is something wrong?'

'My car's not there, Louie,' I said.

'Are you sure that's where you parked it? Maybe you parked around the corner.'

I walked right round the block. There was no sign of my car. Louie was waiting for me.

'You find it, Mike?'

'Naah, it's gone.'

'You mean they stole your car from right in front of the precinct?!'

'Looks like it,' I said.

'Whaat?' Louie was almost screaming. 'What kind of creep would do that?'

I had never seen Louie look so mad, and I felt a fear set in. I could see that he was angry that someone had the nerve to steal a cop's car from right in front of the precinct. He was storming up and down, yelling and swearing. I said, 'I want to pray for the guys who stole my car. I don't want to have this resentment in me. Let's pray for them.'

I didn't look at Louie, I just lifted up my hand and prayed. When I'd finished I saw Louie look at me before he turned round and marched off to his car. I had to go back into the precinct and report my stolen car. Then I had to do all the paperwork. I'd done it plenty of times before, but not for my own vehicle, and that did make me mad!

I was off for the next two nights after that so I didn't see Louie. I knew he'd been upset, and I figured it was best to leave him alone to calm down anyway. I went back on duty that Sunday night. I was in the locker room getting my uniform on when Louie came in.

'Hi, Louie,' I said, 'how you doing?'

He sat down on a bench before he answered. Then he looked at me.

'I told my wife what happened the other night with your car,' he said.

'Oh yeah.'

I could imagine what she said, that she would think I was

crazy too, but I knew he was waiting for me to ask so I said, 'Well, what did your wife say?'

'She said, "You couldn't do that, Louie, pray for someone like that. You couldn't pray for anyone, let alone someone who stole your car." And she's right, I couldn't. What is it, Mike? What's made me like this? Is it what we see all the time?'

'It's mostly that, I guess,' I said, 'the stuff we have to deal with every day. We all feel fear and depression. We see our guys die young, getting shot or shooting themselves or drinking themselves to death, but you know what, Louie, there is hope even for us. I know you're a good man, Louie, I know you mean well, but you were in Vietnam, you've done twenty years in this job. I often wonder how you've lasted so long, how you've kept your sanity.'

'I haven't kept my sanity,' he said. 'Often I cried alone. What's the answer, Mike? I know you're happy.'

'Louie, there's only one truth,' I said, and I shared with him about Jesus. 'Look, Louie, we have a prayer meeting at our house on Friday evenings. Why don't you come along? We're a friendly group of people. Bring your wife, no pressure, you can see what it's all about.'

'I'll ask Laura, see what she says.'

The next night he came in and said, 'Okay, Laura and I'll come to your prayer meeting.'

That Friday, after the praying and the Bible study, we had an altar call and Laura and Louie were the first two to raise their hands for salvation.

A few weeks later, Ann and I took them upstate for a weekend. We often did that, took cops and their wives away for a couple of days to chill out and relax. On the Saturday afternoon we went for a walk and we came across a beautiful clear river running through a valley.

'Hey, Mike,' Louie said, 'why don't we go in there and you can baptise us?'

They were both real excited, so the four of us waded into

162

the river and Ann and I baptised them both. As Louie went under the water, I looked up at the sky. It was a sunny day without a cloud anywhere to be seen, and it felt like heaven opened and Jesus smiled down on us. Even walking home dripping wet couldn't spoil it for us. Louie and Laura grew in their faith and today they are still committed Christians living in upstate New York.

Time and time again, I see God make good out of bad. If my car hadn't been stolen, it might have been a lot longer before Louie and Laura came to know Jesus.

And having the car stolen turned out to be good for me, too, in a completely different way. I'd only bought the car three weeks before it was stolen. I'd paid $600 for it, and when I insured it, to save money I only took out minimum insurance coverage. When it was stolen I notified the insurance company just to inform them, but shortly afterwards the insurance man phoned me back.

'I've checked your policy – you are covered for theft.'

'No, I can't be. I didn't ask for that.'

'Well, we must have transferred your old insurance. Whatever, you've got it.'

I didn't argue, I figured he must know what he was talking about, and insurance companies aren't famous for offering more money than they need to! When the cheque arrived it was for $800. Ann and I danced round the kitchen blessing the Lord that day.

Over the years I often looked forward to my retirement. I'd think, 'One day this will all be over, all the killings and suicides and violence,' but it always seemed a long way off.

I was sitting in the van one night when the Holy Spirit told me that it was time to leave the police force and go into full-time ministry. I didn't do anything right away: I wanted to make sure it was a word from God. Two days later, I was certain that this was what God wanted from me now. I had already done more than I needed in order to be able to retire, but I'd hung on until God said it was time for me to go. At the end of my tour of duty that night, I went into the office and handed in my papers. It was like a weight lifted from my shoulders.

On my final tour of duty I went down to the locker room in the basement to change into my uniform for the night. As I dressed I kept thinking, 'I'll never do this again – never put on this uniform, never see myself in uniform in this mirror again, never have to do this again. This part of my life is almost over.'

I wasn't afraid of the future but I knew that there were people I would miss. I went out on the van for the final time and completed my last tour of duty, then I went back to the precinct. There was nobody in the entrance foyer or at the desk, which was unusual, but I made my way back down to the locker room to change out of my uniform for the final time. It took me almost thirty-five minutes – there were so many thoughts and memories running through my head, making me pause from time to time. At last I was back in civvies. I emptied my locker, put all my things in my bag and headed out. As I got to the door, I stopped in front of the mirror for a final time. I remembered the very first time I'd looked at myself in my smart new uniform, and I could see twenty-two years pass by.

'You got older, Mike,' I said to myself.

I walked back up the stairs to the foyer, and there was a crowd of guys standing there. I knew some from other districts; some of them had retired. I didn't know what was going on. Then Billy came out of the crowd. We'd been in police academy together. He put his arms around me and his cheek next to mine. I could feel the tears running down his face. He let go of me and looked at a piece of paper he had in his hand, then he crumpled it up and threw it down.

'Aaah, forget that,' he said, and he started to share his

memories of me and our times together. After he'd finished, one by one the guys came up to me. Some gave me a hug, some were crying, others gave me a wink. They were all tough guys showing their emotions. I realised again that not only did I love them but they loved me. Money can't buy that kind of friendship.

After I'd spoken to each of them in turn and said goodbye, I finally left and got in my car and headed for home. As I was driving over the bridge into the Bronx, I started to cry a little about the good people I was leaving behind. It had been a tough twenty-two years and I knew I was doing the right thing now, but there was still a little sadness in my heart.

I hadn't told Ann that I was retiring; I was keeping it as a surprise for her. That morning, when I got home she was in the kitchen as usual making breakfast. I gave her a little hug, then I said, 'Ann, I got something to tell you.'

She was leaning over the table and she looked up into my face. Sometimes the news I had for her wasn't good.

'What's that?' she said.

'I retired.'

She looked at me, making sure I was serious and that she hadn't misheard.

'It's true, Ann, I retired today.'

With that she collapsed, right down on to the table. I grabbed her and helped her back on to a chair. She started crying, and I realised what it meant to her. It showed me what she had gone through for twenty-two years, the pressure she had lived under. She was crying, but she was so happy and she looked at me as if she still couldn't believe it.

'The work's not finished yet, Ann, but God is going to lead us in a different direction.'

We sat and talked, remembering the early days, passing the police test, graduating, how happy we'd been, and the bad times, and Jesus coming into our lives.

'Whoever would have thought, Ann, when we first started

our Bible study, that God would have done all this with our lives, that he would have used us to bring so many people to know him?'

Just about every cop that I worked with for any length of time was saved, and there were countless others, many whose names we didn't know, who'd made commitments to God.

'This part of our life might be over, Ann, but God has so much more in store for us.'

I've been out of the force for more than ten years now, but sometimes when the phone rings I still think, 'Oh, no,' and I pick it up expecting to hear the words, 'Hey DiSanza, you've gotta come in today, we're short of men and there's a riot.' That's the impact all those years had on me.

Chapter 17

My time in the police department was made up of a whole series of incidents, some major, some minor, some good, some bad. I sure have plenty of memories.

Like the time I was in the locker room, putting on my uniform, when Bobby, one of the other cops, came in. He came over to me and asked me a question about Jesus. I was always pleased to have the chance to talk about my best buddy so I sat and talked with him for about ten minutes. When I'd finished, I asked him if he'd like to receive the Lord.

'No, not right now, I'm not that interested, thanks, Mike.'

He left then. I wasn't too disappointed. I'd had a chance to share my faith and I figure no words about Jesus are ever wasted. I stood up and started to make the final adjustments to my uniform, when Frankie appeared.

'Hi, Mike.'

'Oh hi, Frankie, where'd you come from?'

'I was sitting in the next aisle. I heard you talking to Bobby.'

'Oh yeah?'

'Yeah. I was wondering, Mike, d'ya mind if I ask you some questions?'

'Course not, Frankie, whadya wanna know?'

He went on to ask me some things about God and, before I knew it, he'd received Christ as his saviour. I'd thought my task that day was to talk to one guy, but God intended the words for another. And Bobby's time will come!

Then there was the time I was walking down 86th Street in Manhattan, when suddenly I heard a lot of whistling. A few minutes later I saw the reason for it. A lady strolled out of a side street, naked except for a pair of very high-heeled shoes. She was a nice-looking lady but she needed some help. I walked over to her, put my hand on my hip and she hooked her arm through mine. 'Hi cutie,' she said. 'Hi honey,' I replied, 'let's take a walk down here,' and I headed us in the direction of the nearby hospital. When we arrived at the hospital, the nurses came out, put a hospital gown on her and led her into the waiting room. Nobody in the hospital, not the nurses, the doctors, or the clerks, was at all fazed by her appearance. In a smaller town, a naked lady walking in might have caused a stir, but in the Big Apple it was just another day.

Another day I had to go on duty right after attending a funeral. I was wearing my best suit, and as I walked into the precinct catcalls and shouts of 'Who's that handsome guy?!' greeted me.

The sergeant asked, 'Hey, Mike, what you doing all dressed up?'

'I was at a funeral.'

'Who died?'

'One of my brothers in the Lord.'

'You still into that God stuff, then, Mike?'

'Yep, Sarge. Once born again, always born again.'

I got changed and went out to my post. I had just stopped in a restaurant for a break when another cop came in. I recognised him from the district but I didn't know him well. Guys came and went regularly. Some cops stayed in the same district for years, others just passed through. He saw me at the table and he came over.

'Can I say something to you?' he asked.

'Sure.'

'I was in the precinct this morning when you arrived. I liked the way you weren't ashamed to tell the guys that you were at a funeral for your "brother in the Lord". I thought it took a lot of courage.'

'Aw, the guys know me well. I must have witnessed to them all over the years.'

'Can I talk to you, ask you a few things?'

He started to share about some of the problems he had, the main one being that his wife had left him. After we'd talked, I said, 'Why don't we pray, ask God to restore your marriage?'

'Do you think he will do that?'

'I don't know, but let's pray and hope he does.'

I grabbed his hands across the table. He pulled them away.

'Don't be embarrassed,' I said. 'You told me you thought I was brave. Well, now's your chance to be brave. Don't worry about what people passing by think.'

A couple of weeks later he came up to me again. 'I just want to thank you for praying with me that time in the restaurant. My wife's come back to me. I told her about us praying and she said, "That's nice. Maybe that's what we need to do: start praying instead of fighting all the time." '

I hope they're still praying together.

The morning rush hour is real busy for any cop in New York. One morning Hank and I were on patrol together. We knew the caretaker at one of the Broadway theatres, and after the rush hour he let us into the theatre for a ten-minute rest. We sat in the seats, took our shoes off and put our feet up. It was warm and dark in the auditorium, and we must have closed our eyes for a second because the next thing I knew I was aware of bright lights and the sound of clapping. I opened my eyes and looked around. There were some ballet dancers on the stage and people in the seats. I nudged my partner. 'Hank, wake up,' I whispered.

'Whad? Whassamatter?'

'We're in the theatre and there's a performance going on around us.'

'What?!'

We both sat up and looked around.

'We'd better get out of here.'

We tried to creep out, but as soon as we started edging our way to the end of the row everyone started laughing, so we stood up, took a bow and hurried out of the theatre.

'Sorry, guys,' our pal the caretaker said, 'I forgot there was a preview performance of *The Nutcracker* going on today.'

'Well, why didn't you wake us?'

'Aah, you looked so peaceful sitting there!'

Anyone who worked with me any length of time knew not only of my faith in Jesus but also the way I seemed to have a special protection. They knew there were times when I should have been killed but I wasn't, even though I never wore a bullet-proof vest. People thought I was crazy not to wear one, but I knew God had promised to protect me and my faith was in him.

I relied on God every day for everything. Each time I went on duty I said, 'Please, Lord, don't let me have to kill anyone today.' And I never did. I was involved in plenty of dangerous incidents, but I finished my career without having to take another human being's life, and I thank God for that.

My fellow cops knew there was something different about me, and if they had problems they'd ask me to pray for their families or about the situation they were in. There were often miraculous answers to those prayers.

Back in the locker room at the precinct, one of the guys asked me to pray for his son. He was very seriously ill and about to go into hospital for an operation. 'I'm real worried about him, Mike, will you pray for him?'

'Sure, Tony, we'll do it now.'

'Now?'

'Yeah.'

'Well, okay, but I don't want everyone to see us. Let's go behind the lockers.'

'Sure, if that's what you want.'

We held hands and prayed for a miracle for his son.

A few weeks later I met Tony again.

'My son ain't sick any more, Mike. He's doing great. Thanks for that prayer. "The man upstairs" is becoming more real to me every day.'

'That's great, Tony, and maybe one day you might call him by his real name – Jesus.'

At one time there were a number of organisations in New York that were trying to publicise their particular causes by threatening to bomb public places. There had been a number of small explosions, and the police department was on full alert. Grand Central Station was one of the targets, and a contingent of plain-clothes cops was ordered to patrol the area around it, keeping an eye out for suspicious individuals. I was one of those on duty on New Year's Day. It was coming up to dinner time and I was just radioing my partner, Ed, to suggest we take a break and go eat when a well-dressed guy came up to me. He was walking two poodles, each wearing its own cute little red coat. 'Are you a policeman?' he asked me.

I guess he'd spotted the radio and figured out that we were undercover cops. I nodded.

'That means the mayor must have got my letter. I wrote to him about a robbery that happened here two weeks ago, and he's sent you to check it out. That's wonderful.'

We'd been told to keep quiet about the purpose of our patrol to avoid alarming the public, so I just smiled and let him think his letter to the mayor had worked. He was so pleased it would have been a shame to disappoint him, anyway.

'Did I hear you say you were going to eat now?' he asked.

'Yeah, that's right, it's time for our meal.'

'May I buy you dinner?'

'Nah, that's okay, we'll just go find something.'

But he persisted, and at last I agreed. He said, 'If you and your partner go to that garage, the serviceman will take your order.'

I called Ed and we went into the garage – and this was a garage like we had never seen before in our lives. The cars were magnificent, and the floor was covered with plush carpet. It was better than the apartments many people had to live in in the city.

We dined like kings: I had a filet mignon and Ed had extra large shrimps. It was a real New Year feast for two ordinary New York cops.

One of the officers I worked with was a Jewish boy called Arty. He and his girlfriend were in love, but they weren't sure whether they should marry because she wasn't Jewish. He talked to me about it one day.

'You know my girlfriend's a Christian, Mike?'

'No, I didn't, Arty. Is she truly committed?'

'Yeah, she's born again.'

'Praise the Lord. But what about you, Arty?'

'No, I'm not, Mike, I don't want to lose my Jewishness.'

'God wouldn't want you to lose your Jewishness either. After all, the first Christians were Jews.'

I went on to share a little more with him and then I gave him a tract to take away with him and read.

A couple of days later I saw him again. He was grinning at me.

'Hi, Arty, what you been up to?'

'I've been in trouble with the police, Mike, thanks to you.'

'Whadya talking about?'

'Remember we talked and you gave me that tract? It was warm when I got home that day so I decided to take some of my clothes off and lie on the bed to read it. So I was lying there in my underwear when God touched my heart. I was so excited that I ran outside and did back flips in the yard. That's when my neighbour called the cops.'

'And they were real understanding, I bet!'

'I was so embarrassed, I didn't know what to tell them.'

Luckily the police let him off with a warning, and a few months later Ann and I joined in the celebrations at his wedding.

Yeah, I have a whole heart full of memories.

Chapter 18

So now I was retired. At last I had a chance to relax, relieve some of the pressure of all the years in the force, catch my breath. Those were my plans: the Lord had different plans for us.

The first thing we did was to move to Florida. I'd been feeling that the time was right for us to start a Cops for Christ ministry in the southern part of the United States, and you can't get much further south than Florida. The area also has the benefit of much lower taxes than New York, and if I wanted to continue with my ministry I needed to make my pension stretch as far as I could.

So, a month after retiring, Ann and I and our four children packed up our belongings and set off for Florida. We had bought a piece of land in Inverness and had a house built. It was hard to leave New York, with all its memories and our friends, and the rural citrus county of the west coast of central Florida came as a culture shock to us city dwellers. We didn't know a single person there when we arrived, but they were an open and friendly bunch who responded well to a smile or an outstretched hand. We soon got to know people and made friends.

One guy we met was another retired NYC policeman who was very interested in the ministry of Cops for Christ. He became secretary of the first chapter we set up. There were maybe seven officers and a couple of their wives present at our first meeting in Brooksville, but within a short time news spread throughout Florida and more chapters were set up, from Miami in the south through to Pensacola in the north. From there it spread to California and all over the northwest of the country.

Then one day I had a phone call from a friend. He was leading a team of about a hundred young teenagers to do street work evangelism in Bogota, Colombia, and he wanted me to go along and do some witnessing with them. I felt the Lord moving in this and I agreed to go.

Carmen, who's a popular singer in America, had written an exciting musical piece entitled 'The Champion', and the young people performed a drama to this several times each day on the streets of Bogota. In it, Jesus and the good angels are fighting against the devil and the bad angels, with God as the referee. All the young people were in costumes, and it was a great performance. At the end of the fight Jesus is lying on the floor, and God starts to count him out – 1, 2, 3. He gets up to 9 and Jesus rises and grabs the devil and throws him down. God then holds up Jesus' arm and declares him, 'The Champion!' Hundreds of local people gathered each time to watch the young people put on this drama, and at the end the whole place would erupt, with everyone cheering and very excited: thousands were saved.

We were in Bogota for twenty-six days altogether. After about twenty days of evangelism, we were tired and drained and we needed to be ministered to ourselves. We went to a meeting to hear a Colombian Christian sharing his testimony. His name was Eduardo. A former gang leader, drug lord and murderer, he had been saved while he was in prison. When he came out, he started a ministry in Cartouchio, a small section of Bogota that was also known as Streets of Blood. In Cartouchio, within a five-mile area there would be on average four killings each and every day. When God led Eduardo to Cartouchio, Eduardo was concerned because many of his former cartel enemies were still in the area. One night soon after he arrived in the town, a gang burst into his apartment and fired at him, but not one bullet hit him, and Eduardo knew then that he was assured of God's protection. He started evangelising and set up a church in Cartouchio, and at the time that I first met him he was running two houses, one for young men and one for young women who were ex-addicts, former killers, ex-prostitutes and recovering alcoholics.

I was interested to hear Eduardo's story. It fascinated me that someone with his background should have been saved. While he was speaking, I felt the Lord tell me to get to know Eduardo. 'I have a ministry for you both.' I didn't want to do anything too quickly in case it was just my own thoughts – I wanted to check that this really was the Lord speaking to me. And anyway, this was really the last thing I wanted to hear – my life was already very busy and I didn't need another new ministry. So I sat and listened and figured the Lord would confirm it if it was right.

As soon as Eduardo finished speaking, he jumped down from the podium and ran straight to our group. We stood out from the locals, as a large number of the young people in our group were blonde and blue-eyed. Through an interpreter, Eduardo asked, 'Which one of you is the New York cop?'

It turned out that Eduardo had been told about me. Fascinated to hear that a cop could be saved, he wanted to meet me. I liked him immediately. He was in his early thirties, a happy-go-lucky kind of guy, bold for Jesus, not worrying about what people thought of him for it. I still didn't want to get too involved so I didn't say anything about a ministry, but at the end of the meeting I gave him my number and told him to call me if he was ever in Florida.

That night we all went back to the complex we were using in Bogota and went to bed. While the kids were sleeping, the Holy Spirit told me to get up and pray for Eduardo. I got out of bed and dressed and walked round the building, praying in tongues. The Holy Spirit shared with me that I would hear from Eduardo again and that I should keep praying for him.

It was four months later, when I was back home in Florida, that I received the call from Eduardo. My heart leapt when I realised who it was. God hadn't forgotten about the ministry he had in store for us. When Eduardo invited me to Bogota to preach I didn't question it, because I knew this was God's plan. I did have to work out when was the best time to go and I also wanted to talk to Ann about it. I wasn't sure how she'd feel, but she was excited when I told her.

'Oh, Mike, remember the prophecy? This is the final piece.'

The prophecy Ann was talking about was one I'd had early on in my police career. It was at the time that I had to choose between staying in the police force and giving it up for full-time ministry. Then the Lord said to me, 'If you stay a year on the police force, I'll give you a city; five years, a nation; and if you spend your career there, I'll give you nations.'

By the end of my first year as a police officer, I'd completed my probation and I'd seen many lives saved in New York City. After five years I was preaching all over the United States with Cops for Christ. And now, after twenty-two years on the force, my ministry was taking me to other nations.

'You're right, Ann,' I said. 'God is true to his word.'

I made the necessary arrangements and flew to Bogota as soon as I could. Eduardo picked me up from the airport in his broken-down old car and drove us to Cartouchio. It was one of the poorest areas I've ever seen in my life. The streets were littered with garbage, there were thousands of homeless people wandering around, and drug addicts were shooting up in full view of everyone. It looked like a lost society. Even after my experience in New York it was a shock, but I wasn't overwhelmed. I had seen God do so much in bad situations in NYC that I knew he could work even in Cartouchio.

Eduardo and I started preaching on the streets. We declared Jesus' name with boldness and many people were saved. It's not like Europe or America, where most citizens have some knowledge of Christianity. In Colombia many different gods and idols are worshipped, and have been for centuries. But when we prayed for people, we could see them being released as their demons left and the peace of God came over them. I've read stories in the Bible of people being freed from demon possession, and here I was seeing it in reality. I was experiencing a new dimension of God's power as he released and healed people. There was much violence and evil in the city but 'where sin increased, grace increased all the more' (Romans 5:20).

When it was time for me to leave I told Eduardo I would love to have him come to the States and minister there.

He shook his head sadly. 'It is not possible,' he said. 'Because of my criminal record, I am not able to visit your country.'

'I didn't realise that, Eduardo,' I said. 'It would be so good if you could come. Your story would touch many, I'm sure. Let's pray about it, ask God if there is a way.'

When I got back home I sat down and wrote a couple of letters, one to the Colombian Embassy in Washington and one to the American Embassy in Bogota. I told them I was a retired cop from New York City and a good friend of mine wanted to visit me. I explained about Eduardo and how I believed that his story, of how he'd changed from being a gang leader who intimidated others to a man who dedicated himself to helping others, would be a great help and encouragement to many young people. The letters must have been well received, because soon after that Eduardo told me that he'd been given a permanent visa to leave Colombia at any time.

A year or so later, I had another phone call from Eduardo. He wanted me to go to Colombia again. He explained why. Eduardo was one of seven children, and each one of them had committed murder. His father had been jailed for murder. At one time, his mother was the only born-again Christian in the family. God had told her that she would see her whole family saved. Now three of his brothers, his father and one of his sisters had all become Christians through Eduardo's ministry. Only one sister and one brother remained unsaved.

'Jesus has put it on my heart,' Eduardo said to me, 'that my brother, José, will be won through Mike.'

I knew Eduardo well enough to know that he wouldn't make something like that up. I had respect for him and I knew he wouldn't say that unless he was sure it was from God. I wanted to go, but the airfare was $800. I talked to Ann and we shared the problem with a number of people who knew about Eduardo's ministry and supported him in it. Between us all, we managed to raise the money for the airfare, and off I flew again.

Eduardo met me at Bogota, and with Hector, the interpreter, we got into his car and headed off for Medellin, where José lived. The journey took us along the only road through the mountains. It was narrow, windy and rough, and while we were travelling two of our tyres had blowouts. The people there are used to tyres blowing, and at frequent intervals along the way there were tyre centres so we were able to get them fixed quite easily.

Then, about three-quarters of the way there, a bomb went off just ahead of us, causing a rockslide that blocked the road. Eduardo stopped the car sharply and soldiers in full uniform came running down from the hills and surrounded us. I looked out of my window to see a soldier with his semi-automatic rifle pointed straight at me. He didn't look me in the eyes but stared at a point just to the side of my face. Eduardo muttered something quickly and quietly to Hector, then he got out of the car and marched up to the soldier who appeared to be in charge. Hector leaned forward and whispered into my ear, 'Don't say anything.'

I figured Eduardo didn't want them to know that I was an American. I couldn't understand what the army was doing, stopping us under these conditions. If they wanted to question us, they could have made us stop without using a bomb. I was puzzled, but I knew the peace of God and I wasn't overly worried.

Eduardo and the soldier continued their discussion, waving their arms at each other, raising their voices in the typical Colombian way. At last, after about thirty minutes, Eduardo returned to the car and we drove away. I looked back over my shoulder as we left and saw more soldiers arriving in a truck. They jumped out and started firing at the first bunch, who ran away up into the hills. Eduardo kept his foot down on the pedal and we soon left all the commotion behind.

'What was all that about?' I asked. 'Why did the army stop us and what was the shooting about?'

Eduardo grinned, 'The first soldiers weren't from the army but were guerrillas. They like to think they're in charge on the hills. And if they'd known you were a New York cop they'd have taken you up to the mountains and held you for ransom, maybe cutting off your fingers and then your toes.'

The NYPD had been responsible for the arrest of many Colombians involved in drug cartels, and it would have been sweet revenge for them to catch me.

Eduardo began to laugh.

'What's so funny?' I asked.

'God knew what they would do, and he spared us.'

Just as we arrived in Medellin, another bomb went off in the bank. Several people were killed and many more injured.

'I feel like I'm back in New York,' I said. 'I haven't been here a day yet and already two bombs have gone off!'

Eduardo's brother José ran his own autobody shop, and Eduardo took me there to meet him. He spoke good English, so after Eduardo had introduced us he and Hector left us alone. It had taken us about thirteen hours to travel from Bogota and I was exhausted. I sat on a chair and put my feet up on

José's desk. He looked at me, amazed. 'That's okay, make yourself at home,' he chuckled.

'Thanks, I'm just so tired,' I said.

I asked José a little about himself. 'How come you speak such good English?'

'The US government gave me a scholarship to study at a college in the States. I was training to be a plastic surgeon.'

'So how come you're fixing cars now?'

'I got mixed up with a drug cartel and ended up in prison. I was in Rikers Island for five years. When I came out, I'd lost my scholarship and they deported me back here.'

We carried on talking. José was friendly but slightly apprehensive. After a while he said, 'Mike, are you one of those reborn Christians?'

'You mean, born again. Yeah, I am.'

'You seem different from the rest.'

'What do you mean different?'

'You've been here for about twenty minutes and you haven't told me I'm going to hell. Most Christians, it's the first thing they tell me.'

'Why do you think you're going to hell, José?'

'Look, friend,' he gestured round the walls, 'look at all these pictures.'

It was a typical repair shop with lots of pictures of naked women and cars on the walls.

I said, 'Do you really believe these pictures will send you to hell?'

'That's what everyone tells me.'

'José, you could have pictures of Snow White and the seven dwarves up on your walls and still go to hell.'

For the first time I noticed that José kept his eyes firmly focused on me.

'What do you mean?'

'I mean you could have pretty pictures up on your walls and still go to hell.'

'I don't understand.'

'You're not going to hell because of dirty pictures. The only reason a person goes to hell is because he hasn't received atonement for his sins through Jesus.'

José was staring at me now and his eyes began to water.

'Can you tell me that again?'

'José, Jesus isn't waiting for you to elevate yourself, to put yourself right, because you'll never get there on your own. He loves you where you are right now.'

The tears started to roll down his cheeks.

'Mike, I want what my brother has, but every time I try to do the right thing, I do the wrong thing.'

I shared with José then a little about Paul's experience as he writes of it in the Bible.

'Paul, the great apostle, had the same problem. He said, "I don't do the good I want to do; instead, I do the evil that I do not want to do" (Romans 7:19, Good News Bible). He found out he couldn't do it on his own.'

'So what's the secret formula, Mike?'

'There's only one way, and it's not secret. It's to admit that you're lost and that you need a saviour.'

We prayed together then, and as we prayed I could see his countenance change. When we started he was very nervous and anxious, but as he was set free his face took on a look of deep peace.

We went outside to find Eduardo. The brothers hugged and then Eduardo hugged me and shook my hand. He said, 'Thank you, Mike, thank you for coming.'

'How long are you staying in Colombia, Mike?' José asked.

'Well, as it cost such a lot to get here, I figured I'd stay for a couple of weeks in Bogota and do some ministering while I'm here.'

'Would you mind if I came with you?'

'What about your business?'

'They can run the business without me for a couple of

weeks. I'm so happy, I just want to come with you.'

It was wonderful to see José so on fire for the Lord so quickly. Eduardo was delighted, and we all piled back into the car and set off on our long journey to Bogota again.

As we drove back through the mountain pass where the guerrillas had stopped us, I felt the Lord nudge me. I said to Hector, 'Tell Eduardo to stop the car.'

Eduardo pulled the car on to the side of the road.

'What's the matter, Mike? Why are we stopping here? It's not a good place to stop.'

'Why are we allowing them to frighten us with their bombs? Why don't we go up there and witness to them?'

Eduardo had no fear of death; he'd been through so much in his life.

'Okay,' he said, 'let's go for it.'

'Are you nuts?' José asked. 'I know those people. They'd as soon . . .'

'Quiet up, José,' I said. 'You can stay here if you want to, but we're going up there.'

José laughed. 'I've been a Christian for less than a day and you got me going out to dangerous places to witness. Okay, I know a pastor that lives up in that village. I'll take you to him.'

We drove off the main road along a bumpy track up the side of the mountain. When we reached the village the pastor came out to greet us. He was very excited when he heard that José had met Jesus. He and his small church had been praying for revival and they saw our arrival as an answer to prayer.

Eduardo carried microphones in his car, so we got them out and started doing some street evangelism. The people living in the village had a tough life, working hard for just the bare necessities, and they came out on to the streets to listen to what we had to say.

We preached a simple salvation message, that God knew how difficult their lives were and that there was a better place.

People who have to endure a lot in their daily lives always want to hear that there is something better, so great crowds gathered and many were saved.

We prayed over many in the name of Jesus and saw them fall to the floor in tears as demons left them. José was watching, unable to believe what he was seeing. He knew many of the people who were being saved, and as they were released by the power of God he was jumping up and down and yelling, 'He was a drug lord!' or 'He was a hitman!' It wasn't our sermons that saved these people, but God working through believers to break down strongholds that the devil had maintained for centuries.

Over seventy people were saved in that village. Not only that, but the pastor and his church were encouraged to continue. When we'd turned off the main road to go up into the mountains two days earlier, we had no plan; the Holy Spirit gave us the people, and God did the deliverance.

We said goodbye and made our way back to the road to Bogota. When we arrived at Eduardo's mother's house she heard the car and came out to greet us. José got out and his mother fell to her knees and screamed. Just by looking, she could see the difference in him. No one had called her to tell her that he was saved, but she knew. Eduardo joined his mother, and together they knelt and thanked God. They must have stayed on their knees praising God for a good hour.

It isn't unusual in those parts of the world for people to spend a long time in prayer, but by now we hadn't slept properly for days and all I could think of was sleep. Eduardo's mother couldn't do enough for Hector and me. She offered us food, but all I wanted was to wash and go to sleep. Eduardo gave me some soap and I went and stood under the trickle of water that passed for a shower in their humble home before crawling on to the mattress on the bare floor. Hector washed and took his place on the other mattress in the room, and I was soon drifting off.

Just as sleep was coming over me I opened my eyes. I sensed something in the room. I looked up, and in the doorway stood a woman. She was in such a rage that saliva was drooling from her mouth. Hector was awake too by now, and I said to him, 'Who's that?'

'It's Eduardo's sister. He told me she has terrible rages.'

'Hector, start talking to her about Jesus.'

The more he talked, the wilder she became. At last I asked Hector to call her over to us. She moved closer, snarling at us all the time.

'Hector,' I said, 'tell her God forgives her for anything she's ever done.'

I believed that was what God wanted to say to her, and as I talked Hector translated for me.

'Tell her that he understands where she is right now and he wants to release her, and she wants to be released, she's waiting to be released, but she can't believe that God can ever forgive her for what she's done. Tell her that she's got to believe that God is listening right now, and he says, "I forgive you." '

With that she got down on her knees and cried. Hanging on to Hector's legs as he prayed over her, she asked God for forgiveness.

So now Eduardo's mother's prophecy had been fulfilled: each member of her family was saved. There was great rejoicing in the house that day.

Eduardo's sister is still part of his church, which has two hundred and fifty members, mostly from the streets of Cartouchio and all on fire for Jesus. Many have gone on to minister themselves in different areas of Colombia. Eduardo now runs seven houses for young men and three for young women, and his church has its own building to meet in. Eduardo continues to minister all over South America, the States and Canada. There is no government money available in Colombia for his work, so he relies on donations from supporters to fund his ministry. Each time a new house is opened, the police department in Bogota donates beds and bed linen because they have seen the effect of his ministry in the town formerly known as the Streets of Blood. They know the difference it's made.

As for me, my visits to Colombia were just the start of my international ministry.

Chapter 19

There was no mistaking the sound. It started on one side of the room and spread to the other: I was being booed. In all the meetings I'd addressed, all the places I'd spoken, I'd never ever had a response like it. I turned to the man sitting behind me, the man who'd organised the evening, and hissed, 'Dave, they're booing me! What have I done?'

He grinned, 'You've upset them a bit by what you said, that's all.'

'But how? I only said, what, ten words? How could I upset them in ten words?'

'It only takes one word, Mike, just one word.'

I stared at Dave Sansome. He and his wife Dinah had invited Ann, our kids and me to Britain on behalf of Victory Outreach, an organisation that houses and works with young people who've had trouble with the law or with drugs or alcohol. Dave and Dinah are doing a really great job. We were to speak at some local churches and prisons. This particular evening we'd driven to a big Pentecostal church and Dave had introduced me. I'd stood up and said, 'It's great to be with you tonight here in England.'

And that's when the booing started.

'So what's the one word that's upset them so much, Dave?'

'England, Mike – you're in Wales, not England, and the Welsh are none too fond of being mistaken for English.'

I turned back to the audience.

'I'm sorry, I didn't know! I'm from the Bronx, we love everybody in the world!'

I stretched out my arms to encompass everyone, and they started to laugh. I'd broken the ice, and things were okay from then on. God had gotten me out of another tricky situation! I really hadn't realised that we had crossed a border travelling from London. In America you have to travel thousands of miles before you cross a border to Canada or Mexico, and then it's obvious. I wasn't expecting to drive a few miles along a road and be in a different country!

But it was in Wales that we had one of our best experiences.

Dave had arranged for me to go into one of the prisons to speak. Ann wasn't planning on coming but Dave suggested she should go in with me. To my surprise, she agreed without hesitating, even though I knew she wasn't too sure about it.

If I'd ever pictured a British prison, it would have looked like this one – very old, with solid, concrete-block walls – really depressing. The young offenders were kept separately from the adults and we were leading two Sunday meetings for the different age groups. The first one was for the teenagers. Ann and I sat with the chaplain at the front and the chairs were arranged in rows in a semi-circle around us – I felt like we were in a wagon train surrounded by Indians. As I waited for the youngsters to take their places I marvelled again at what God can do: here was I, an ex-policeman, going into a prison. I could have ended up in prison for quite different reasons if God hadn't stepped in and rescued me. And there are plenty more of us who should be in there but who didn't get caught.

There must have been eighty or ninety young people

gathered there for the service that Sunday morning. The chaplain said he'd never seen it so full. I figured they'd dragged themselves out of bed because they wanted to see a real-life New York cop.

The chaplain introduced us and Ann shared some of her story. She has a great rapport with young people, and they listened attentively. When it was my turn, I told them about some of the violence and trouble I'd experienced and how I'd been saved. Then Ann asked if she could pray. When she'd prayed she said, 'When you go back to your cells, think about what you've heard here this morning, and if you feel you'd like to know more about Jesus, read John's Gospel in the Bible.'

We had brought in some Bibles to give out to them, and at the end every one of those boys came over to us and hugged us, some of them in tears. We hadn't preached at them but the power of God had been at work.

The next service was for the adults. I felt some unease because Ann was in there with me, concern about possible danger for her – after all, I was a cop and it was cops who had put these guys inside, so they could well resent my being there – but God quietened my anxiety. The chaplain said to Ann and me, 'Shall we do it exactly the same way? I felt the presence of God, you felt it and they felt it.' So we went through it again, and at the end all eighty men lined up to thank and hug us. As we left, Ann said, 'Isn't it amazing how God has blessed us in this?'

We don't know how many were saved that day, but it was a beautiful experience and I was reminded of my Christmas visit to Rikers Island Prison and the good things that came out of that. God truly can work in the most unlikely situations.

The next part of our trip took us to Italy. Michael, our eldest son, had stayed at home in Florida to work, but the other three children, Douglas, Rachel and Jonathan, were with us. The trip to Europe was taking five months altogether, so between us we had a load of luggage. It had been arranged for someone to pick us up at the airport in Rome. Unfortunately, the gentleman who'd volunteered hadn't been told there were five of us plus luggage. He showed up in a little Fiat automobile, and when he saw us he was quite upset. He started shouting and waving his arms around.

'Whoa,' I said, 'I don't speak Italian, slow down.'

I had a phrase book, and between us, going through the book very slowly, we managed to make ourselves understood. Our driver went and made a phone call and we sat down to wait. Two hours later another two cars arrived and we were transported safely to our destination.

Rome is a fantastic city. We took the kids sightseeing – the Colosseum, the Sistine Chapel and all the ancient buildings – and we had a great time. It was in Rome that I met one of the finest Christian guys that I have ever known. He was an Italian police officer who was very interested in Cops for Christ and he set up a number of meetings for us. He loved God, he loved us and took care of us, and he was serious for the gospel. He was part of a charismatic group of churches and was responsible for pastoring about nine churches by himself.

From Rome we were taken to Sicily by Paul Schaeffer, a Canadian director of the 'Christ is the Answer' missionary team for Italy. They had a missionary team in Sicily at the time, and I was due to speak there. We stayed on the island for four weeks and during that time we saw many people saved and delivered.

One of the police officers from Sicily, a guy called Vincenzo who was starting a Cops for Christ chapter, took a month off work so he could drive us everywhere we needed to get to. One day, with the 'Christ is the Answer' team, he took us to a small town called Vittoria, and we started some street evangelism. We had an interpreter with us who translated as we spoke. On hearing our accents, crowds began to gather, as there is a really good bond between the Italian and the

American people. Some came out from their apartments on to their balconies to listen to us.

While Ann was giving her testimony, I noticed a girl in the shadows. My eyes kept going back to her. I could tell by the way she was standing that she was listening attentively, but she had a coldness and a stiffness about her. When it was my turn to speak I felt God say to me, 'Direct your message at her but don't look at her. Don't single her out but let what you have to say be for her.'

I told the story of Mary Magdalene, the prostitute that God had delivered, and at the end I said, 'God held nothing against her but he forgave her for all her past life. Is there anyone here who would like to receive Jesus, to know God's forgiveness for all their sins?'

The girl came out of the shadows and crawled across the street. Grabbing Ann's ankles, she hung on to them, soaking them with her tears. She told us that she was a prostitute and that she wanted to ask Jesus into her life. We prayed with her and she was saved. Right away she gave up her former life, joined the 'Christ is the Answer' team and was discipled by them. I was reminded of Lydia, a character from the Bible who lived in the Mediterranean area. Her life was changed when she responded to the apostle Paul's message. Two thousand years later, in the same region, God transformed another young woman's life. Yesterday, today and for ever, he is the same.

Everywhere I go I get to experience miracles. That may sound like boasting but, like Paul, I say, 'Let him who boasts boast in the Lord' (2 Corinthians 10:17). God keeps giving me miracles because I'm obedient to him. I have a simple story and I keep going. Life is hard – it's not all hallelujahs – and my story is about how to deal with life. I don't give up because I think I've blown it. I just get up and get on with it.

Vincenzo was very excited at all the things he saw happening in the mission and at the churches. Consequently, one evening he invited us to his home to have a meal. He invited his whole extended family, it seemed. The table was huge and the meal delicious. After dinner I shared a little of my testimony and Vincenzo's father-in-law was saved. It was a great night – Vincenzo was so happy, he couldn't stop dancing around the kitchen – and afterwards his father-in-law joined us at all the tent meetings.

It was a huge tent, like a circus tent, seating up to about six hundred people. One night I was sitting on the platform waiting for my turn to speak when the director of the mission came up and whispered in my ear, 'There's a telephone call for you, Mike, from America.'

His words made me a little anxious. I wasn't expecting a phone call and I feared it might be bad news: my mom had been sick before we left, and Michael, my eldest son, was still in the States too. I was praying as I went to answer it.

'Hello,' I said, apprehensively, 'this is Mike DiSanza.'

'Hi, Mike, it's Joe Lalotta, remember me?'

I had to stop and think for a minute and then it came back to me. In March of that year Ann and I had visited our old home church in New York. It's a Pentecostal church with Sunday morning attendance of about two thousand people, and I go back there a couple of times a year. On my last visit, in March, I had told them about our forthcoming trip to Britain, Italy and Sicily, and after the meeting a man had come up to me. He'd introduced himself, saying he was a cop in New York, that he'd been saved for about four months and that he'd like to go to Sicily with us. The fact that he was a cop had created an instant camaraderie so I'd said, 'Yeah, sure you can come. Just get the air fare together. We'll find a place for you to stay with the mission team and you can certainly help evangelise with them.'

'When are you going?'

'The plan is that we leave some time in September. Ann, the kids and me are going to be travelling round for about five months, but I don't know the details of where we'll be yet.'

'Okay, I'll call you before that to make the arrangements.'

The months went by and it was soon time for us to leave, but Joe hadn't called. I didn't think too much about it as I figured that he'd changed his mind. Now I was in Sicily and he was calling me.

'Joe, yeah, I remember. Hey, man, we're here. I'm sorry I didn't call you before we went.'

'That's okay, it was my fault, I thought you'd said to call in September. I phoned your house and your son gave me your number. Is it okay if I join you now?'

'Yeah, sure, if you want to.'

'I'll be on the plane tomorrow.'

I was amazed: here was a guy who'd been a Christian for about seven months, and he was willing to drop everything and fly out to Sicily. Getting a last-minute plane ticket isn't cheap either, but he was so anxious to be here with us.

We picked him up at Palermo airport the next day. Joe knew that the 'Christ is the Answer' mission moved around the island and he asked, 'Where are you staying right now?'

'Vittoria.'

'Oh my Lord,' he said. 'You know why I wanted to come on this trip with you, Mike? Partly I wanted to get involved with Cops for Christ, but partly I wanted to come to Sicily because all my family come from here originally and I wanted to come and tell them I've met Jesus. I've never met any of my family because I was born in America, but both sets of grandparents came from Vittoria.'

Joe's grandparents were dead now but he knew he had many aunts and uncles and cousins who still lived in Vittoria. He didn't know their addresses, though.

'Mike, will you come with me tomorrow and help me to look for my family?'

'How can I say no, when you've come all this way to tell them about Jesus?' I grinned. 'But I've gotta tell you, Joe, the day after tomorrow Ann, the kids and me leave Sicily, so we haven't got much time.'

Joe slept well that night, and the following morning he and I and Tierri, the interpreter, set off round the streets of Vittoria. We walked down street after street, looking at mailboxes and asking people if they knew anyone called Lalotta. By lunchtime we were exhausted and we stopped to rest.

'I don't know, Joe, this is impossible. Do you know how many people live in this town?'

But Joe wasn't listening to me. He was staring at something just behind my head. I turned round to see what he was looking at. It was a mailbox with the name Guiseppe Lalotta on it.

'Guiseppe,' I said, 'doesn't that mean Joseph?'

We went and knocked on the door, which was opened by a woman dressed from head to toe in black. She looked at us sceptically. Tierri explained who we were and that Joe was looking for his lost family, and her face cleared as things clicked into place.

'You mean you're Joey Lalotta's boy, come all this way from America?' Tierri translated for us. 'Oh, come in, come in.' She grabbed Joe and pulled him into the house. Tierri and I followed. The room was full: there must have been fifty people there, all dressed in black. There was great excitement when the woman, who turned out to be Joe's cousin, explained who he was. There was much hugging and kissing and fast Italian talking and gesticulating.

When I had a chance I asked, 'Why is everyone in black? Has someone died?'

'No, not yet, but soon,' the woman said. 'My grandmother, Joe's great-aunt, is upstairs. She is very sick. She doesn't have long to live.'

She took the three of us up to the bedroom. The woman in the bed looked very old and frail. She was in a coma and her eyes and cheeks were sunken into her face. Joe walked up close to the bed and sat beside his grandfather's sister. He took her hand and held it in his. I didn't want to intrude so I went and stood on the other side of the room, but then I heard the Lord say, 'Why don't you go pray for that lady?'

'Oh, no, I don't even know her. I don't want to barge in playing the big hero, trying to make her better.'

'What's the matter, don't you have any faith?'

Right then I didn't, not for healing for the old woman. I wasn't sure it was God speaking and I was scared. Then Joe came over to me.

'Mike, I feel we should pray for my aunt.'

'Wow, Joe,' I said. 'I felt the Lord telling me we should do that. Let's do it then.'

I asked Tierri to explain to people what we wanted to do. One of the old woman's sons spoke a little English, and he said, 'You want to pray for my mother?'

'Yeah,' I said. 'The Bible tells us to anoint the sick with oil and pray for them. Is that all right?'

He understood and was quite happy to have us pray for his mother. It isn't a problem getting oil in an Italian household – there's more than enough of it. He brought us some from the kitchen; we anointed her and prayed. There was no great miracle, she didn't leap out of bed, but then I hadn't really expected her to. I left Joe and Tierri staying with Joe's new-found family, and I went back to join Ann to finish packing as we were heading off for Naples the next day.

I didn't see Joe again for a couple of months. Then, just before Christmas, the pastor of our old home church invited Ann and me back to report on our journey. We shared a little of what had happened in Europe, and afterwards Joe came up and spoke to us.

'How'd it go, Joe,' I asked, 'after we'd left?'

'Fantastic, Mike. I stayed for two weeks, helping the "Christ is the Answer" team, handing out tracts, sharing my testimony. It was great. But the best bit was my family. You remember my great-aunt?'

'Your great-aunt? Ah, Joe, I met so many people I don't remember her.'

'Well, you remember we found my family and my great-aunt was very sick?'

'Oh, yeah, I do remember now. What happened? She died, I guess?'

Joe grinned.

'No. The day after you left, I was sitting in the kitchen, and all my relatives were there with me, all still dressed in black, when this little old lady walks in. I was so excited to be there with all the family that my mom and dad had told me about that at first I thought she was just another one that I hadn't met yet, but then I saw the looks on the faces of all my relatives. I realised it was my great-aunt, the one who'd been in a coma, the one who'd been on her deathbed.'

'Naah! What happened?'

'She remembers us praying over her when she couldn't move or say nothing, and then she was better – and God did that!'

'Wow,' I shook my head, 'that's amazing.'

I'd had so little faith I'd expected her to die.

'And that's not all, Mike,' Joe continued. 'All my family, all my aunts and uncles and cousins prayed for Jesus to come into their lives. They came to the mission tent every night, and each night they got more filled and more excited!'

'That's amazing, Joe. You see, when God up in heaven saw that you, who'd just been saved seven months, were willing to go all the way to Sicily to tell your family about Jesus, he said, "Wow!" and he gave you your family.'

It was a beautiful story Joe told me, and I knew it had to be God at work for everything to fall into place like that.

Chapter 20

I keep in contact with Eduardo in Colombia – I've helped arrange for him to minister in the United States and Canada, and one day, if we can raise the funds, I'd like to get him over to Europe – and in 1998 he invited me to minister with him again. I bought my ticket and I was all set to go to Bogota.

Then one morning about two weeks before I was due to leave, I got up from bed, went downstairs and sat in front of the television; I like to know what's going on in the world. I picked up the remote control and had my finger on the button ready to switch it on when I heard a voice say, 'Go to Northern Ireland.' The voice was so clear and loud that I jumped up. I figured my son was playing hookey from school and hiding behind the sofa, having some fun with me.

'Okay, Jonathan, come out,' I said, 'I know you're there.'

There was no reply so I leaned forward and looked over the back of the sofa: there was no one there. I was puzzled; I'd definitely heard a voice. I sat down again and switched on the television. I had it set to the CNN news channel and the first item that came on was a report of a bombing in Northern Ireland. I felt sure now that it was God speaking to me, telling me to go to Northern Ireland, but I wasn't sure why. I didn't know anyone there, and anyway I'd already bought my ticket for Bogota and I couldn't afford either the money or the time to go to Northern Ireland as well.

I couldn't get it out of my mind, though, and then I recalled a pastor I knew in the Republic of Ireland. His name was John and I'd met him through Ann. She'd been back to visit her parents one year and had attended a Sunday meeting. Afterwards he'd introduced himself to her and she'd told him a little about the ministry of Cops for Christ. Through Ann, he invited me, if I was ever in the area, to go and speak at his church. A year or two later we went to Ireland and met John, and I agreed to address a meeting – and at it six people were saved. I thought of John now and I called him up on the phone. As I dialled his number, I realised it would be about lunchtime in Ireland and that John would probably be out at work. The phone only rang once before it was picked up.

'Hi, John,' I said.

I have a very recognisable New York voice and John immediately knew who it was.

'Mike, how are you? We were just talking about you. When are you coming to Ireland again?'

'Well, John, that's why I'm calling you.'

I told him what had happened and asked him, 'You're the only person I know over there – do you have any contacts in Northern Ireland?'

'Sure, I do, I've got a good friend called Jackie who works up there.'

'Could you set up some meetings for me?'

'Call me back and I'll see what I can do.'

A couple of weeks later, I changed my airline ticket from Bogota to Dublin and went off. Another of John's friends, an associate pastor called Christy, drove me to Belfast and introduced me to Jackie McKee. His vision was to set up a Teen Challenge type work in Northern Ireland, and to use youth to bring about restoration and break down the barriers of sectarianism. I used my first trip there to get to know people and learn a little about the problems. I didn't know all the particulars, but I was certain that God loves everybody and his desire is that no one shall perish but all come to know Jesus (2 Peter 3:9). While I was there, they took me to see the wall that separates Catholics from Protestants in one part of the city. It's a sad sight, but I know it's not people that we have to wrestle with but powers of darkness. Only the forgiveness of people and the love of God can break down that wall.

My short visit left me with a desire to go back again, and a year later I was booking another flight. This time I was accompanied by Bobby MacIntosh, a real good friend and gospel singer, and Guy Salerno, another retired New York cop and a good friend of mine from way back. Guy and I had worked together many years earlier but we'd lost touch with each other. One day a few months back, I had come home from visiting a friend and my daughter said, 'Guy called.' She gave me his number; it had a New York area code.

I said, 'Guy? Guy who?'

I knew one Guy but he wasn't in New York. Then I remembered, 'Guy Salerno! It must be. Gee, I haven't seen him for twenty years.'

'Well, he asked if you'd give him a call.'

'Sure, I'll do it now.'

I dialled his number; the phone rang a couple of times and then a familiar voice answered.

'Guy, hey, it's Mikey.'

'Mikey, it's great to hear your voice again after so long.'

We exchanged news and then I said, 'Guy, how'd you get my number?'

'It's an interesting story,' he said. 'I was driving home from work late one night when I was stopped at the lights. A man crossed the street in front of me, looked into my car and suddenly rushed round to the side and knocked on my window.

You know how it is, you can't be too careful in a big city late at night, so I peered at him before opening my window. Then I realised it was Bill Eller.'

Bill was in police academy with me, and he'd worked with both Guy and me over the years.

'Wow,' I said, 'you mean Bill recognised you in a car in the dark? Most people crossing the street just want to get to the other side as fast as they can, they don't stop to look in cars!'

'That's not all,' Guy said. 'When I realised it was Bill, I pulled over to the side so we could talk. We reminisced a little about old times, and I asked if he had seen any of the guys. Then Bill said, "Yeah, I hear from Mikey Di." I said I'd like to get in touch and he said, "Wait a minute, I might have his number here in my wallet." And he did, and he gave it to me, and you know the rest.'

'And Bill happened to have my number on him? That's amazing!'

Guy said, 'It was no coincidence that I met Bill. That light coulda changed a second earlier and we'd have missed each other.'

We talked some more and I told Guy I was planning a visit to Ireland and Wales.

'I've always wanted to go there,' he said. 'Can I come with you?'

'Well sure, Guy, but you know, I'm going to be visiting churches and I'll be busy. I don't know whether you'd enjoy it.'

'That's okay, I'd like to come anyway.'

It would be good to have him on the trip, but he wasn't a Christian and I wasn't sure how he'd deal with all my ministry. Still, he was eager to go, so I gave him all the details and left him to buy his own ticket.

So now the three of us, Guy, Bobby and me, were in Northern Ireland.

Bobby needed to get to meetings early so he could set up

his equipment and check the sound levels. I usually accompanied him. One evening I was sitting quietly, waiting for the service to begin and listening to Bobby tuning up, when a big guy came into the church. He must have been over six foot two and 280 pounds. He looked at us, without a smile on his face, and said, 'I came two hundred miles for this meeting: it had better be good or there's going to be serious trouble.' Bobby and I looked at one another.

The meeting started and I watched the big guy as Bobby was singing. He had his head bent down, but every now and again he looked up at particular words in the song. After he'd sung, Bobby shared a little of his testimony – how he'd been a drug user, how he'd attempted suicide and how he'd been set free. The big guy was listening intently now; I could tell Bobby's story was hitting him right between the eyes. When I gave the altar call, he was the first one out of his seat. He came out to the front and stood right in front of Bobby for prayer. Now Bobby's about five foot six and he had to look up at this guy. I could see that he was thinking the same as me – if this wasn't good there was going to be serious trouble. Bobby reached up and placed his hand on the guy's shoulder and the big man fell to the ground instantly, touched by the power of God. He was saved that night.

I couldn't help laughing. It could have been us on the floor that night, knocked out by a blow from the big guy; instead, God knocked him out. Awesome!

At another meeting we met an American girl who was living in Northern Ireland. She was very touched by Bobby's songs, especially one called 'Dreamed we were in heaven'. She cried as she shared with us afterwards that she hadn't talked to her mother in America for over a year. Bobby said, 'I don't know what happened to make you have a falling out with your mom, but nothing is so important that it should break up your relationship with her.'

The next night, the girl was at the meeting again. She was

a changed person. She had called her mother, and they'd both cried down the phone and had started to work out their problems.

At that meeting, as usual, I did an altar call and people came up to be prayed for. I finished praying with one woman, and as she moved away I was surprised to see Guy step into her place.

'Hi, Guy,' I said, 'How you doing? You gotta problem? Only I'm supposed to be praying with people who wanna ask Jesus into their lives.'

'I want to ask Jesus into my life.'

'You want Jesus in your life?'

'Yeah, I've seen you and all these people and I want what you have.'

Whoopee! Guy had come to Ireland for a vacation and he'd been saved. Thank God that traffic light didn't change. Guy getting saved still brings me great joy today.

Many people were blessed at the meetings, including some former members of paramilitary organisations. At one particular meeting we had both Catholics and Protestants, and as we shared our testimonies we could see that people from both sides were touched. The power of the Holy Spirit was so real that we could see strongholds being broken down before our eyes.

From Northern Ireland we travelled to South Wales. Christy, who I'd met on my earlier visit to Belfast, was now a pastor of a church there and we were going to minister in his area.

One night we got back to our hotel and Bobby and me were lying on our beds when Bobby switched on the TV. We watched the pictures come on the screen of a never-ending stream of people, carrying as many of their belongings as they could, wearily making their escape from Kosovo. Among them were hundreds and thousands of children.

'Gee, I feel for those kids,' Bobby said. 'Wouldn't it be great if we could go to Kosovo and help them?'

I looked at him.

'There's a war going on out there, Bobby. I don't think it would be possible for us to go, and, anyway, what could we do in a situation like that?'

'I don't know, but I feel the Lord wants us to go.'

'Okay,' I said, 'why don't we pray about it?'

Sitting up on our beds, we grabbed hands and prayed. Afterwards I remember thinking, 'Oh well, we prayed. That'll keep Bobby happy.' I didn't think there was any possibility of us going. I should have remembered that you gotta watch what you pray for – you might just get it!

The next day Bobby happened to mention to Christy what we'd prayed and Christy said that he'd been thinking and praying about the same thing. A couple of days after that there was a call from a local businessman who offered a truck-load of brand new clothes if we could get them to Kosovo. I still didn't think it would be possible for us to go. Two days later the shipment of clothes arrived at Christy's church building. People from the church came and unloaded it, and soon the whole place was full of box upon box of underwear, socks, jogging suits, dresses, jackets, all sorts of things. I could see now that God was serious about this, but there was still a problem.

I was due to fly home soon. Ann had been over and joined me for a short while, but she'd gone back to Florida. I called her up and told her the situation. Right away she knew that it was God sending us.

'You gotta go, Mike.'

'That's what I hoped you'd say,' I said. 'We've been given an old police paddy wagon we can use to transport us and the goods, but it'll cost us a lot to get over there, what with the ferries and the diesel fuel we'll need.'

'How much do you need?'

'We figure it will cost about $4,000 to make the trip.'

'I'll phone round, see what I can do.'

Ann contacted some people she knew who were supporters of my ministry, and I phoned some churches. Between the States and Britain and Ireland, we managed to raise the money in just four days.

Meanwhile, other stuff was arriving at the church: toiletries, bedding, toys and more clothing. There were collections in local shopping centres and schools. A team of volunteers worked on the van (which we named Angel), getting it ready for the trip. It was the most fearful-looking vehicle you would ever want to see. We painted big green crosses on the sides and top, which we hoped would identify us as humanitarian aid providers and keep us safe from bombing.

We eventually left Wales at ten o'clock on a miserable rainy night. Three Brits and a Yank, we were setting off on the biggest adventure of our lives. Bobby, who'd started the whole thing off, had been called back home at the last minute because of business, and Guy had only had two weeks' vacation from work so he'd left as well. I was going with Christy and Grip and Brian from the Elim church in Port Talbot (who'd both only been Christians for about six months).

We drove across to Dover and crossed the channel into France. From there we travelled through Germany into Switzerland. We made slow progress because the bus, which was very heavily laden, had a maximum speed of forty miles an hour, or maybe fifty if it was going downhill. As we went up and down the mountain roads through the Alps, there were times we thought Angel wasn't going to make it. We had a few of these conversations:

'You looked in your rear-view mirror recently, Christy?'

'Why's that, Mikey?'

'We've got a bi-i-i-ig line of traffic behind us!'

'Well, the pedal's already on the floor. If I put my foot down any more, it'll go right through.'

'C'mon, Angel, you can do it,' we all shouted encouragingly.

And creaking and hissing, Angel would pump more bitter smoke into the bus, making us cough and causing our eyes to sting.

At last, against the odds, we made it to Italy. It was raining when we arrived at the border, and the bad weather must have upset the guards because they refused to let us through. The officer on duty wanted to know what we were doing. We told him and he shook his head. He couldn't make the decision whether to let us through or not; instead, he called for his sergeant. About an hour later the sergeant showed up. We explained it all again to him. He thought about it, shook his head, and called for his captain. Another hour went by before the captain turned up. He was a sharp-looking military man with a row of medals across his chest. I thought that he was probably in every war Italy had ever fought to earn all those medals.

'Where are you going?' the captain asked.

'To Kosovo.'

'Why are you going there?'

'To take humanitarian aid for the children.'

'I don't know if I can let you go through.'

I was getting fed up by now and I pulled out my policeman's badge. I was still entitled to carry it with me all the time, even though I'd been retired for a number of years now. I waved it in the captain's face.

'I'm a policeman too. Retired. We're part of NATO.'

At least, America and Britain were, and we were American and British. It impressed the captain, anyway.

'NATO? What you got in those boxes?'

'Semi-automatic weapons,' I replied, kidding with him.

'NATO, go. Go on, go.'

He waved us through quickly. We didn't hang around to explain the joke.

We headed for the Adriatic coast, where we were to catch a ferry to Greece. At this time America and Britain were bombing Serbia and there was a lot of tension in the atmosphere. Some people were not happy to see us. We tried to explain that we were there to help the refugees and that we didn't want to take sides, but as the bombing continued the feelings towards us were not good. On the ferry we joined the queue in the café for food. We'd paid our fares and we were entitled to a meal, but they refused to feed us. It was only the intervention of the captain of the ferry that got us anything to eat. As we ate, we could see the men watching us and hear them talking. We didn't understand what they were saying, but we figured it wasn't nice things about us!

We were glad when the voyage was over, but our troubles were only just beginning. That night, in Thessalonica, there happened to be a big crowd of demonstrators protesting about the war. They surrounded our bus and banged on the windows, chanting, 'NATO, go home!' We weren't able to move until the police showed up and held back the crowd, allowing us to get through safely. As we made our way through the Greek mountains, it was scary to see the graffiti freshly painted in red on walls and the sides of hills, 'Clinton is a baby killer,' and 'Yankees, go home.' We realised how much hatred there was towards us. We all prayed that God would keep us safe.

We travelled all night until, in the early daylight, we reached the Macedonian border. There was a big queue of traffic waiting to go through the border checkpoint. When at last it was our turn, they looked at our papers and signalled that we should pull the bus over to the side.

'What's the problem?' Christy asked.

'He doesn't have a visa,' the guard replied, pointing at me. 'He needs a visa to come in.'

Britain is part of Europe so the other three didn't need a visa, but because I was American I did. We tried explaining why we were there and the aid we had and how we just wanted to help people, but this guard kept shaking his head. 'He must have visa.'

I said, 'Oh, Lord, what can I do? I don't want to be responsible for us being turned back now, but I don't want to be left behind, either, not after having come so far.'

I felt the Lord say, 'Go tell them you're a policeman.'

I wasn't sure what good that would do, but I guessed it wouldn't do any harm. There was a mini police station at the border, so I went up to the guard standing outside it and I said, 'I'm a policeman too, ya know.'

'You are policeman? Where?'

'New York City.'

'*NYPD Blue*!' he shouted and turned and ran into the police station. (*NYPD Blue* is a series about cops in New York that has been very popular when it was shown on television.) Next thing, the whole police contingent inside came flying out. One of them was a female lieutenant.

'I always want to hug a New York policeman!'

'Okay,' I said, 'give me a hug.'

We both laughed and she hugged me. Then she asked me what we were doing and what I needed. I told her, and not only did she give me a visa but she also sent two police cars to escort us through Macedonia to protect us from bandits who were hijacking aid trucks. Next thing we knew we were at the Kosovo border. Sixteen days earlier we had prayed, and now here we were on the edge of Kosovo with all this aid. Only the Lord could do something like that.

Now all we had to do was to find out how to get into the refugee camps. We met a pastor who was ministering to the refugees. He was a gypsy who had been saved twenty years before. He was a poor man, but everything he had he was giving away. He was very excited to meet fellow Christians and told us he knew the places to go, but we still had to get things squared with the authorities. We were there for a couple of days trying, but not managing, to get over the border. Then who should we see walking out of the border station but the female lieutenant who'd fixed things for us at the Macedonian border! For the eight thousandth time in my life, I knew that God was in control. She spotted us and came over. 'Mike, what is wrong? Why are you still here?'

'We're still waiting for the authorities to let us cross.'

'Wait here,' she said.

She walked back into the station and came out with three official-looking men in smart suits. She pointed to us and they spent some time talking. Then one of them came over, and said, 'Follow us.' He got in a car and led us to the British authorities, who were patrolling the border. The two soldiers on duty, both carrying semi-automatic weapons, came out to greet us. We told them who we were, where we'd come from and why we were there. They looked at Angel.

'You came all this way in that?'

They were amazed, couldn't believe that we'd made it.

They opened the gates, and at last, nine days after we'd left Wales, we drove into Tent City. Suddenly we were in the very centre of everything that we'd seen on TV and read about in the papers. We could hardly believe it.

Around the time we were there, it looked as though a major war could be brewing. Russia was very unhappy with the bombing, and the Chinese Embassy in Belgrade had been hit so the Chinese government was making threatening noises as well. At night we slept in Angel, and we could look out and see the sky light up as the bombs were going off.

The refugees received us very warmly and we were able to oversee the distribution of the goods we'd brought. We met two Muslim ladies. They were schoolteachers who were refugees themselves, but they'd set up a tent to try and help others. They were very pleased when they saw the clothing we were giving out, and we hit it off well. One of the women told us her story. She said, 'I have two children, a boy of six and a girl of three. While I teach, they are in a day-care centre. One day the Serbian army came. They entered the school and took control of the surrounding area. They forced us all to run for our lives. There was no time to negotiate – we had to run. I ran till I reached the border of Macedonia. I still do not know where my children are. I came back to help others and to look for my children.'

Many seemed to be in the same situation. Every time a coach pulled into the camp, people would crowd around it, trying to see if their relatives were on board. Most were disappointed.

Through the lady schoolteachers we were able to meet many of the leaders in the camp, and we were invited into their tents. In one tent we met seven Muslim men. We sat and shared with them for about three hours. At the end, Christy asked if any of them would like to receive the Lord Jesus Christ as their saviour. Through their weeping and wailing, each one of them received Christ. In the week we were there, we spoke to gypsies, Muslims and those of other religions, and we won many for the Lord. Even out of bad things, God can bring good.

On the journey back, I was sitting in the corner of the bus one night when the Holy Spirit said to me, 'You just pulled a great coup on the enemy. You owe nothing to any man. Don't ever worry about what people think.'

I felt an even greater sense of peace come upon me, and it has stayed with me to this day. We'd been like a little army going in to capture the guns of Navarone. We'd been in, done our work and got out before the devil even knew we were there. There were times when we could have been in real trouble, when serious threats were made against us because of the bombing, but we knew the peace of God.

When we got back to Wales, we had just $6 in our pockets. God had supplied exactly what we had needed for the trip.

It was time for me to go back home to Florida now, but I felt the Lord say to me, 'Go to New York, tell the people there about your trip.'

I said, 'Lord, I've got a ticket to Florida – although that's already overdue.' I was booked on a flight back a couple of weeks earlier.

The Lord said, 'Don't worry about that. Go to New York.'

I had to catch a train to Gatwick airport from South Wales. I was heavily laden. Ann had forgotten one of her suitcases when she'd gone home, so I had that plus my own two bags and a carry-on bag. The train I was to travel on was full when it pulled into my station, and I had to stand. Each time we stopped, more people got on, and because it was late at night many of them were drunken youngsters. Some of them were argumentative, and it looked as though a skirmish might break out at one point. Then someone noticed the New York Police baseball cap I was wearing. That started them asking me questions and distracted them from fighting.

When I eventually reached Gatwick I found there was a shortage of trolleys to carry my luggage on. The terminal I had to get to was about a mile away so I had to make the journey in relay, taking one bag a hundred feet, going back, getting the next, and so on. At last I reached the check-in desk and I handed in my ticket. The attendant looked at me like I was crazy.

'This ticket is for Florida. It's out of date. And you're telling me you want to go to New York?' he said.

I just kind of sighed and looked at him.

'This ticket is out of date!' the clerk said.

'Yeah, I know,' I sighed, 'but there's a good reason for that.'

I went on to explain what had happened, and a bit about our trip. The clerk listened, then he said, 'Hold on a minute,' and he went back into the office. When he came out again, he had his supervisor with him. He asked me to explain about our trip again. The end result was that they gave me another ticket to New York and a ticket from NY to Florida. It must have been worth about $900 all in. The Lord sure was taking care of me.

I arrived in New York on a Saturday. Bobby MacIntosh

picked me up at the airport, and after we'd talked some about the trip he'd missed, he took me to the movie house to see the new *Star Wars* film that had just come out. I slept right through it.

The next morning we went to church. Bobby had already agreed with the pastor that I would share with the congregation something of my trip, and I told them some of the miracles God had performed. I stayed in New York for about three days, and in that time almost $7,000 was raised for Kosovo. When I got back to Florida, I collected another $3,000. It was the most money I'd ever raised in my ministry, and I mailed it all to the gypsy pastor we'd met over there. After a couple of weeks I contacted him to make sure he'd received the cheque okay. It hadn't arrived. For six weeks we couldn't track it down. We got on to the Chase Manhattan Bank, who found out where it had been held up, straightened it out and got it, at last, to the pastor. Praise God!

Since that first time, Angel has made a number of trips to Kosovo, and Christy has been provided with a warehouse to store the clothing and medicine that is still being collected. The last I heard, Christy, with the aid of the Elim Fellowship in Europe, has set up housing and a centre for medical aid in Pristina. Although the war is over, it is still a volatile area and the need is huge.

One night after I got home, I remember sitting talking with Ann. 'Who would ever have thought it possible?' I said. 'Who would ever have believed that something that turned out to be as big as this could have come out of just a simple prayer?'

'Well, just look at your life, Mike,' Ann said. 'Look at all the good things that have come out of prayers. Who would ever believe some of the things that you've seen?'

I took her hand.

'God sure is good,' I said.

Postscript

In the course of writing this book, I had cause to go back to New York for a couple of days. I was walking down 6th Avenue one afternoon when I came across a street evangelist standing on a corner, addressing the passing crowds through a microphone. I stopped to listen to him. He could see that I was interested in what he had to say, and when he took a break he came over to talk to me. I told him what I was doing there and a bit of my story. He offered me the microphone.

'Go on, take it,' he said, 'give my voice a rest.'

I took the microphone from him and stepped into his place. I looked around. It was more than thirty years since I had first taken my bullhorn out on to the streets of Harlem. A lot of things had changed. Even in the few years I'd been living away from New York, it was becoming unrecognisable. But some things will never change.

I saw people hurrying by, their faces lined, their shoulders hunched. I lifted the microphone to my mouth.

'Listen up, people, I've got some good news for you!'

Appendix

International Cops for Christ

In 1974 Joe Scarano had a desire to begin a Christian ministry by and for cops. International Cops for Christ was founded, and has been meeting the spiritual needs of cops throughout the world for over twenty-five years through prayer, travelling evangelists, books, booklets, tracts and radio programs.

International Cops for Christ today is being used by the Lord to evangelise around the world. We go into places where only policemen would go. Many of our men and women are evangelising in some of the toughest spots in the world: in the inner cities of New York, Los Angeles, London, Belfast and Milwaukee; in Colombia, Kosovo, Bosnia and Kenya. These are just a few of the places where we are winning souls for Jesus in these last days, pulling them out of the fires of hell. Alleluia! We are also starting many new chapters around the world for International Cops for Christ.

We do street evangelism, and we speak in prisons and in churches and wherever God may open a door. If any church organisations would like us to speak, we are willing and able.

Check out our web-site (www.acopforchrist.com) or e-mail us on MNDCFC@acopforchrist.com.

The Sinner's Prayer

If you want to ask Jesus to be your saviour and forgive you of all of your sins, and to spend eternal life with Him in Heaven, say this prayer:

Jesus, I believe that I am a sinner.
I also believe that you are the son of God
And that you died on the cross and shed your blood for all my sins.
Come into my heart and my life right now and make me a child of God.
I receive you right now as my Lord and Saviour.
I also receive your forgiveness of all of my sins.
In Jesus' name,
Amen